"Five Bells" Job Done

Best wishes
Tony Liddicoat

by

Tony Liddicoat

This second edition was published in 2008 and supersedes the first edition.

T L Publishing,
Leonis,
Paxton Gardens,
Woodham,
Surrey
www.tonyliddicoat.com

© 2008 Tony Liddicoat. All rights reserved.
No part of this book may be reproduced, stored in a retrieval system, or transmitted by any means without the written permission of the author.

ISBN: 978-0-9561399-0-0

Printed in the United Kingdom

This book is dedicated to my grandchild
Poppy Elizabeth

One Sunday morning in 1936 at Le Mourillon, near Toulon, I waded into the Mediterranean and looked into it through fernez goggles. I was a regular navy gunner, a good swimmer interested only in perfecting my crawl style. The sea was merely a salty obstacle that burned my eyes. I was astounded by what I saw in the shallow shingle at Le Mourillon, rocks covered with green, brown and silver forests of algae and fishes unknown to me, swimming in crystalline water.

Standing up to breathe I saw a trolley car, people, electric-light poles. I put my eyes under again and civilisation vanished with one last bow, I was in a jungle never seen by those who floated on the opaque roof.

JACQUES YVES COUSTEAU

Table of Contents

Introduction   13

1963-1971   15

    In the Beginning...   15
    Early Diving   18
    Army Basic Compressed Air Diving Course   24
    Posted to Germany   32
    Combat Engineer Diving Course, Kiel   35
    Army Diving Supervisors/Instructors Course   39
    Combat Engineer Tractor Trials   49
    Kiel, as Instructor   52
    Sunken Armoured Personnel Carrier Recovery   65
    Helicopter Jumps   77

1971-1973   81

    Commercial Diving in Civilian Life   81
    Inspection of One Hundred and Twenty British Rail Bridges   85
    Contract to Repair the Cracks in the Reactor Transfer Tunnel, Winfrith Nuclear Reactor, Dorset   86
    Replacement of the Lock Gate Sill, Penzance, Cornwall   93
    Construction and Anchoring of Pipeline, Holyhead, North Wales   101

1973-1979 **106**

Back into Uniform 106

Re-Qualification in the Army 107

A Struggle to Promote the Cause of Diving 110

Scotland, Part: Adventure Training Teaching the Army 112

Helicopter Recovery, off Portland Bill 115

Kenya, Part 1: Military Diving Reconnaissance 119

Belize, Part 1: Operational Military Tour of Duty 120

Scotland, Part 2: The Blasting of a Deep Water Channel 137

Berlin 155

Kenya, Part 2: The Mombasa Wreck Excavation, 1977 156

Berlin, The Return 183

Osnabruck, Holland, Kiel 187

Conversion to the New Aquarius Military Diving Equipment 190

Mombasa 1979, Phase 2 of the Wreck Excavation 197

Mombasa Summary 207

Back to Osnabruck, Germany 209

Vogelsang, Germany 211

1980-1982 **221**

Posted to the Army Diving School, Marchwood 221

Canadian Combat Divers Course, 1981	230
The Mary Rose Project, Part 1	251
Clouds on the Horizon	253
Belize, as a Diving Instructor	257
The Rescue in Belize.	258
Dick Alba.	270
Back to Marchwood.	273
New Orleans	275
Army Diving, the End	281

1982-2000 — 287

Folkstone, a New Beginning	287
Army Sport Diving Expeditions: Bovisand and Scapa Flow	298
Falkland Islands	307
Harz Mountains, Sardinia and Lake Titicaca	313
Folkstone, Again: A Bit of Philosophy and All that!	321
Falmouth	331
Kiel, with the Herberts!	332
Back to Germany	337
Reassurance and Confidence whilst Training	338
Nearing the End	346
Norway, 1991	347
Bornholm, Denmark, 1995	354
Cyprus	359

Summary **364**

Glossary of Terms and Conditions **370**

Acknowledgements **374**

Introduction

At the time of writing this book, I have been diving for 44 years. It has always been my main thread in life, and I have gained much from it.

I achieved the top in military, commercial and recreational diving. I met many great and not-so-great characters, experienced the whole spectrum of diving, and saw the best and the worst of human nature.

I wish to share some of these experiences with you, and give you an insight to my story.

I hope you enjoy it.
Tony Liddicoat.

List of Qualifications and Dates

1963 Recreational Diver
1967 Army Compressed Air Diver
1968 Army Combat Engineer Diver
1969 Army Diving Supervisor/Instructor
1970 Specialist course, Oxygen Rebreather
1971 Specialist course, Helium Rebreather
1980 HSE Part one certificate
1982 Association of British Diving Schools Commercial Diving Instructor
1981 Canadian Combat Diver
1981 British 'Diver of the Year'
1984 Craft Operator
BSAC Advanced Diver

1963-1971
In the Beginning…

In 1963 I boarded a train at Bath Spa station using a rail warrant given by the Army Recruiting Office. At Corsham I met up with another lad also heading for the army at Dover. Eventually, at Dover Priory station, our numbers had swollen with young lads from all over the UK. I was apprehensive and tense, and was fifteen years and one month old. We were roll called, processed, loaded onto army trucks and taken to barracks on a hill overlooking Dover and the channel. It was the beginning of an adventure and the start of a lifelong passion of mine, for going underwater.

Within weeks we were well in to basic training, which left us exhausted every day. All of our waking hours were fully occupied. There was no free time at all and we had no energy to get up to mischief. By term two we had 'passed in', and either life became a bit easier or we had adapted. We were then informed that we had to select a hobby to attend twice weekly in the evenings, and sometimes on Wednesday sports afternoons. During this time the local sportswear shop was allowed access to us and you could get anything you wanted, on credit. Wow, so you could look through these glossy black and white catalogues and order anything you wanted and acquire it on a signature. You did eventually pay out of a thing called 'credits', which was our unpaid wages that we got to go home with at the end of the term. I bought a dive mask, a simple yellow rubber dive mask, with the glass kept in by a large Jubilee clip-type fitting. The reason for my choice was that the camp had a new twenty-five-metre swimming pool for the swimming team, and I had initially listed one of my practical sports as swimming.

I therefore ended up spending much of my spare time in the pool. However, I suffered badly from chlorine in the eyes, and at the end of any training would look like a panda. So, I thought the mask would give me protection against looking like a drugged-up zombie for hours after swimming. I know you may say that a diving mask does not allow you to do swimming training, but I specialised in breast stroke. By only using my mouth to breathe, I could just about get away with it, but it meant working harder with my arms to ensure my head and mouth were well out of the water for inhaling. However, what the mask did for me in a heartbeat was open the door of the underwater world. It was unbelievable to see all the arms and legs and dropped kit on the bottom. I spent the whole of my first session sitting underwater and watching for as long as I could hold my breath. I was hooked and instantly gave up swimming as a hobby and joined the Sub Aqua Club. The next problem was to come up with an idea that allowed me to keep my head underwater all the time without having to come up for air. The following week I bought a snorkel.

Now, those of you who are unfamiliar with military ways should realise that the Army sometimes makes enjoyable and lovely pastimes as miserable as possible. Diving is just such a pastime. In the belief that instant obedience is the answer to all tricky situations, be it going over the top of the trenches, or searching for bodies in a sewer, the preparation and training for such situations is unsympathetic, often brutal, and certainly no fun.

At that time, the people who ran the sub aqua club in Dover were all military divers, having done the Army Basic Diver course at Marchwood (the army diving school). The only way they knew how to train a diver was how they were treated on their course, and we were inducted the same way.

As a requirement to join the sub aqua club, we had to perform a series of confidence and swimming tests in the pool. There were perhaps twenty of us, all hopeful of joining the sub aqua club. There were all the usual: tread water with clothes on; five hundred metre swim; duck dives to retrieve weights; and, at the end of these tests, we were lined up at the diving boards and told to go singly up to the three-metre board and perform a belly flop.

Sort of startled, 'What?' 'You know, belly flop, hurt yourselves'. Gulp. I remember thinking, 'just the once Tony, that's all, it only stings a little bit, and it will soon go, and then you are in'. I watched as a couple of lads in front of me stormed down the board, only to bottle out at the last second and just jump in feet first. They got the thumbs down and were told to join the queue again or forget about sub aqua. When my turn came I remember bouncing off the board like a swastika in flight with my legs higher than my head. I remember the sting, but thankfully got a thumbs up. That evening only four of the twenty or so hopefuls had qualified to join the sub aqua club. I was on my way.

Early Diving

The next stages of progression were very exciting. Using an aqualung to breathe underwater enabled us to gain confidence quickly by 'ditching and donning' the equipment underwater, buddy breathing, mask clearing (back to being a panda!), and pretend knife fighting (all the rage at the time). We used the army professional diving equipment, which included the Heinke MK V twin hose demand valve, and as a result I got to know the function, repair and servicing of this valve very well. This was to give me an advantage when, in a couple years time aged seventeen, I attended the Army Basic Compressed Air Divers (ACAD) course at Matchwood. (One of the exam questions being 'Draw and explain the operation of the Heinke MK IV demand valve.)

Initially, all the training was done in the pool. We all got better and more confident, but we were still not using diving suits.

I remember a pile of unkempt rubber in the dive store, which turned out to be some well-worn and smelly neoprene diving suits. Most were in a serious state of disrepair. One day we were told to select from the pile a suit to fit us, as we were going to do our first open water dive in Dover docks. The suits proved useless. They fitted where they touched and were hard to get on without ripping. The bootees were like old socks, no hard sole luxury in those days!!

So off we set in a truck to Dover Docks.

The water was pea green and freezing. A shot rope was lowered down at the dive site, and we were meant to dive down it and touch the shot (a fifty-six-pound weight). Down I went, into the dark green and then black water. I then kind of landed in a big soft area and continued to follow the rope, which disappeared into it. It was soft silt, which billowed up and engulfed me, and removed any light that there was by enveloping me in ink black silt.

My ears were hurting like mad, even though I could clear them. I started to follow the shot rope into the silt, which became thick mud. The shot was some five feet under the mud. I heard another diver breathing and stood up, holding on to the shot rope, to be greeted by two big handfuls of silt being pushed into my face and into my ill-fitting suit. This was a hilarious practice of the instructors.

We dived with a lifeline tied around our chests, which was tended from the surface. We communicated on the lifeline by using a series of tugs on the rope called 'pulls and bells'. A pull was a lengthy tug on the lifeline. A bell was a short sharp tug and given in twos (i.e. 'Ding, Ding'). There was a whole raft of lifeline signals, which we had to learn by heart. This again was good preparation when I came to do my army diving course. One of the questions on the basic course was to write down and explain all lifeline signals. I already knew them, and had been using them before I went on the course. Even now, my house is called 'Five Bells', which is the signal for 'Finished Work'.

I received four pulls (to come up) on my lifeline and surfaced up the shot rope. 'Get out, kit off' were the delicate instructions. During the ascent my head pain increased. I was experiencing 'reversed ear' symptoms, due to the high pressure air in my ear and sinus cavities not being expelled quickly enough, and this was causing pressure pains. To be honest, after that dive I had a severe headache for a couple of hours. It was awful and I admit now that if someone had said then, 'Diving is not for you lad – give it up', I would have done so. But nobody did say that, and here I am over forty years later telling my story. But it was that close, believe me.

During the remainder of my time at Dover we dived extensively around the harbour and breakwater. The regiment also had sailing and canoeing clubs. Therefore, there was always plenty of activity in and around the harbour, and we divers always had access to a boat to deliver us to the dive sites.

Amongst the permanent staff were various diving enthusiasts who would occasionally join us for an open water dive. One such person was the Regimental Sergeant Major (RSM) who was like a god. None of us spoke whilst he was around in case we incurred his wrath. He was, however, an OK guy who also happened to be a very rotund Scotsman. An incident I remember well was whilst kitting up out on the breakwater one day. The RSM was sorting through the pile of shoddy neoprene suits and picked out a pair of trousers that looked hopelessly too small. Nobody said anything. We averted our eyes and busied ourselves. The RSM walked into the middle of us and said 'OK, who's going to help me into my suit?' There was a couple of seconds of silence, when this lad piped up 'We all will Sir!' It may not seem so funny now, but I was quite helpless for fifteen minutes. The remainder of my time at Dover saw me gaining confidence and experience. During the summer months we would do up to five or six dives a week.

High water entry into Dover harbour

Step off entry

Exiting the water using the harbour steps.

Getting dressed for diving on Dover breakwater.

Looking back, these were indeed basic days of no lifejackets, mainly twin hose aqualungs and ill fitting diving suits. I remember seeing a large Dungeness crab on one of my first dives, sitting and occupying a car tyre. It was totally bound up in fishing line and unable to move. One of the instructors brought it up. We cooked and ate it. It was my first example of food from the sea. We would dive in all weathers and of course being a walled harbour, there was always a leeside area to dive. The place where I did my first ever open water dive is now covered with asphalt and is a huge ferry terminal. Every time I use the terminal now I think of that first dive. The water was always dark, cold and sometimes foreboding, with visibility on a good day up to 2 feet. It was all good practice for what was to come.

In those days there was no keeping of logbooks or progression through a structured system, which was meticulously recorded. You just dived.

Army Basic Compressed Air Diving Course

At the end of my time in Dover, I 'passed off' on a parade and become an adult soldier. At seventeen and a half years old, the legal age to join the adult army, we were all sent to Aldershot and prepared for being sent worldwide on our first postings. Whilst at this department called 'Holding and Drafting' I was ordered to attend the Basic Compressed Air Diver course No 76 at Marchwood. The course began on the twenty first of March 1966, six days after my eighteenth birthday.

You may remember my earlier comment that the army delights in making normally happy pursuits as miserable as possible. Here we go!

Marchwood is situated across the Solent waterway from Southampton, which in those times was a busy ocean-going terminal. Marchwood was a self-contained military port, as in those days the army were trained to run ports and harbours. Therefore, it had trades like stevedores and dock crane operators. Marchwood was the centre for training all these maritime trades as well as diving.

The port contained a large jetty on which was situated a large dockside crane on rails. On the other side of the jetty was moored a steam ship, called the Stevedore.

The bottommost depths of the Stevedore were used as the divers' changing rooms. These comprised a couple of metal rooms in the hold. There was no light and it was accessible only by a steep metal stairway. The walls and floor were dripping with condensation and seawater brought in by soaking divers. The diving suits (neck entry Avons), cotton undersuits and white seaboot socks were left on the floor after each dive. There were no shelves or seats. It was just a square metal room, which dripped condensation and was permanently wet, dank and dark. This resulted, naturally, in the diving suits and divers' wool and cotton underwear being permanently wet, smelly and cold.

We were introduced to a drill which was used to simulate suspected limpet mines placed on the hull of the ship, and thus required divers to enter the water and start search patterns immediately. The outer limit of time tolerance accepted by the instructors was one and a half minutes from minding our own business in the cook house/classroom/barracks/ anywhere, to divers in the water. The practice was known as 'Operation Awkward', and any time, place or occasion that an instructor said to you 'awkward', a turbo response was demanded from the students. During such drills, not only did we have a single steep stairway as access and exit to the hold changing room, but there was no light and all the kit was just in a large wet pile. We ended up grabbing and dressing with the first suits that came to hand.

Part of the surface swimmers' equipment in those days included a large brass diving knife on a leather belt. This was inherited from the standard helmet diver. The belt would be worn around the waist, whilst the knife and brass sheath would hang loosely swinging from it. The whole thing weighed three or four pounds and would swing around, especially whilst running, and very often clatter you in the nuts.

The answer was to hold it with a free hand to prevent such delicate injury. Very often we would be carrying logs or a boat on our shoulders whilst running, and therefore did not have a free hand.

The practical open water diving training to practice our lifeline signals, hand tools, buoyancy, etc. was done from a diving pontoon situated at the end of the jetty. There would be four or five shot lines along the pontoon, and a diver would be given his own to work from. Although we still used the Heinke MK V valves, most military diving is done using the full face masks, which completely encompass your face and senses. To clear our ears during the dive we wore a spring nose clip, which would clamp your nose shut, and which you could use to blow against to clear your ears.

One of the main advantages of using the full face mask was that if the diver became unconscious underwater, he would be able to continue breathing, as his mouth piece would be held in his mouth by the mask. This would prevent him from drowning, and he could easily be recovered and revived.

Just below the mouthpiece on the outside of the mask was a port opening called a 'spitcock'. This allowed the diver to breath from the atmosphere whilst on the surface and his attendant would switch to cylinder air prior to getting into the water. It saved wasting cylinder air.

The Heinke regulator was fitted with a spring reserve, which operated when the cylinder pressure dropped below twenty-five bars (approx.). This would then allow a spring to push forward a valve with a grooved head onto the air inlet port. The groove allowed a reduced quantity of air to the diver, who would then signal with his lifeline a request to surface and state he was on reserve. It was often an unpleasant experience, likened to breathing through a small hole in your teeth. If, at the time of the reserve kicking, in you were breathing heavily from exertion and out of breath, it was very unpleasant. We had no means of surfacing independently. Most of our pontoon work was done wearing ten-pound lead boots, so there was no bale out. You had to use the lifeline signals.

In addition, we would have been under freezing water for up to an hour with wet undersuits, which were meant to keep us warm. We very often ended up numb from cold. In those days gloves or mittens were not allowed and considered to be sissy. Not only were they not allowed, they were non existent. Very often guys would surface so frozen they could not climb the exit ladder. Some had just topped up fully with freezing water and started shaking uncontrollably. Of course, we would then have to run with our cylinders some four hundred metres to the compressor shed to charge up the set and return to the pontoon where we then stood in the biting wind, attending another diver. Many guys from my course attended from Germany where they were stationed. They had asked to attend the course because it seemed like a good excuse to get back to the UK for a month and see their families and friends. Many of them had never been underwater before and, apart from the brutal regime of physical training every morning, they also had to contend with adapting psychologically to the black cold water. Most of them never lasted through the first week, and even today the basic diving course still has the highest percentage failure rate of any course in the military.

The March and April of 1966 was bitterly cold. Some of the in water skills and training were done in a circular fresh water tank five metres high and some eight metres in diameter. It had porthole windows around it so divers inside could be observed by the instructors. It was used for practising the oxy hydrogen cutting torch, Temple Cox underwater bolt gun and ditch set routine. Each and every time we needed to use the tank, we had to break the surface ice with a sledge hammer. Believe me, working in there with leaky suits, wet thermals and no gloves was a cold experience.

The course was four weeks long and students who passed were entitled to wear the yellow thread divers helmet badge with SW underneath, also in yellow. The SW stood for 'Shallow Water', as our training was depth limited to ten metres.

Surface swimmer waiting in the safety boat.

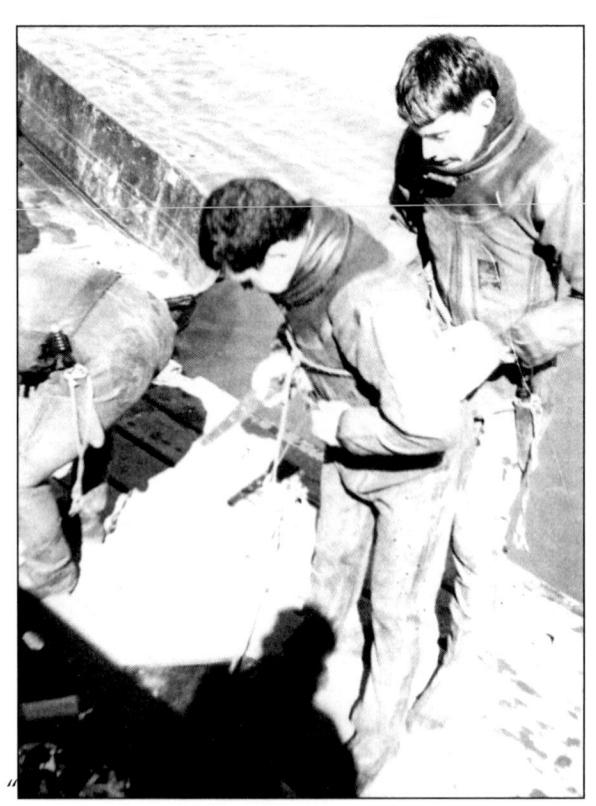

Attendant dressing a diver.

Attendant dressing a diver, note the 'pussers fins'.

Loading the safety boat

We told everyone who asked about the SW that it stood for 'Shark Wrestler' or 'Sea Weed'. I wore the badge with great pride for many years. The course ended with the taking of theory exams. The old favourites of naming and explaining all the lifeline signals and drawing and explaining the regulator, were two of the questions, and the remainder were all about physics: Boyles law, Henrys law and Charles law, etc.

The course attracts its fair share of Special Forces lads. On my course were Dave from the SAS and two lads from the engineer parachute squadron. One of them was a non-swimmer, much to my amazement. However, it was explained to me that you do not need to swim to be a diver, you just commute to your job through the water and commute back. You use the boots to walk or fins to swim, and that is it. It is just like going by bus or tube. They had a point.

I passed the course, came top and received the first ever A grade issued by the diving school for a basic course. (This was told to me by the school itself). Three days later I was on a plane to Germany. I had been posted to Willich, near the Ruhr area.

Posted to Germany

Although diving was my first love, the military classed it as a specialist qualification, and I still had to have another artisan trade. Therefore, I had also trained as a carpenter and joiner, and it was as such that I was posted to Willich.

A strange coincidence happened upon my arrival in my new unit. The only other army diver there happened to be my troop sergeant. As a newly arrived soldier in his troop I was given an initial interview, which was given to everyone. In a heartbeat it was obvious that it was not going to be a meeting of minds. He conducted the interview in front of others. Upon noticing I had recently passed the Army's basic diving course there were a couple of comments from his assembled gallery such as 'Only a basic', and 'No competition Sarge'. It was infantile and taught me that you only get one chance to make a first impression. Thereafter we never ever got on. Sadly, I was to serve alongside this guy later in my career. The higher the rank he became the worse he was, but at least from that first encounter, I knew what to expect.

However, as I later discovered, he had not qualified with the army at Marchwood, but in Hong Kong with the Navy. They took several army lads on a course and gave them the basic diver qualification. The difference in end product between those trained at Marchwood and those in Hong Kong proved to be enormous. Years later, when the system realised this, they instigated a European Water Familiarisation Course. Even now, divers who qualify after a week in warm, tropical waters with lots of visibility and sunshine, bear no resemblance to someone who has qualified in British/European waters. Many of them gave up the qualification when they returned to Europe, rather than re-qualify.

Now, whilst this book is not meant to be about the army, the fact that I am relating my diving experiences initially as a soldier will mean some overlapping.

As I said earlier, during my diving career with the army, I ended up serving directly with this guy on several more occasions. It was a pain. I will not mention his name, but will call him AA if I have to refer to him again.

It was within a month of arriving in Germany that I was told, one afternoon, to prepare for a dive. A soldier at the nearby barracks at Ratingen (near Dusseldorf) had gone swimming and drowned in a water-filled sandpit.

We did a simple grid search from the shoreline out to an aluminium assault boat. I dived first along a jackstay search line. The water was deep and ink black, and to be honest, unless you put your hand directly onto the corpse, you would never find him. Maybe, at this point, I can explain that I was now considered a trained professional military diver, and this occupation sometimes has some quite unsavoury tasks. Recovering dead bodies is such a task, and several times throughout this book you will read of instances of other body recoveries. Like many unpleasant tasks in every walk of life, you would be amazed at how reluctant people become when they are expected to accept responsibility. They are full of excuses, and old war wounds are suddenly crippling to prevent them diving. Such tasks and occasions are a good gauge of your fellow man.

There were four of us in the team searching for the body. Only two of us dived. The body was not found. A few weeks later he floated to the surface and was recovered.

Combat Engineer Diving Course, Kiel

The centre of military diving in Germany was at Kiel, a very beautiful seaport on the Baltic Sea. The British military had a yacht club and a diving unit there. At that time, the diving unit was run by one of the many characters I was to meet. He was a guy called Alec Black, who was an ex-paratrooper engineer and a warrant officer class II. They run a course called the Combat Engineer Diving Course, which was three weeks long. It involved us practising all our engineering and combat skills under water, including a week training at Hameln (the town of Pied Piper fame), practising fast water search techniques in the river Weser. The course was intense, hard work and fun. I did it in September. It was late summer and the scenery was beautiful. The Weser was a formidable waterway, which ran at between two and three knots. It was hard work.

The search, in fast midstream water, involved laying a jackstay with a buoy and an anchor at each end. When the jackstay was laid in the correct position, the divers would be dropped off upstream. They would then swim down with the current to the upstream buoy and pull themselves down the buoy line to the jackstay. By floating backward spread-eagled, facing into the current, you could search a six-foot (two metres) strip along the bottom. Another diver could do the same but hold the jackstay in the opposite hand to the other diver. The searched strip was then twelve feet wide (four metres). The jackstay could then be moved in the search direction by the boat and crew. It proved a good workable system of searching fast water but, like everything, it needed practice.

When you came onto 'reserve' during the search, you were instructed by the boat to swim to the riverbank. As I explained earlier, it was like breathing through a small hole in your teeth, and in two to three knots of water, whilst swimming hard, it was a dreaded experience.

The climax of the course was a 3-day clandestine exercise. We simulated being dropped off behind enemy lines and, working in pairs, we had to liaise with partisans at various rendezvous, where we would be given further instructions and equipment to carry out various tasks.

Whilst I agree with the logic of creating a scenario that physically exhausted us whilst encouraging teamwork, I could not take the role of clandestine diver seriously. This was due to the fact that we used equipment that put exhaust gases into the water. These could be spotted by anyone on the lookout. But we could do a lot as surface swimmers and, as is explained later, by using re-breather equipment and 'over the horizon' drop-offs, much could be achieved clandestinely by divers.

The exercise was fun and sometimes comical. We had been going for nearly two days when we had a rendezvous with a 'secret agent', to accept the delivery of a container of hot stew. It was night, and black, and the stew got kicked over. Nobody had anything to eat. A good lesson, which I still refer to now when teaching survival in my school, is that exhaustion and fatigue make people do stupid things, so always prepare for the worst. Alec Black laughed till he cried.

In the middle of the night we were given 'Op Awkward' and had to place some explosives on a huge set of lock gates. The gates were guarded and floodlit and required all our daring-do and some luck to achieve this. Afterwards, we retired to a safe location and had an hours sleep. After being woken, Alec and the team of instructors got in the truck and left, explaining that it was the last day of the course and that we, the students, had better get back to the diving school ASAP to clean and hand back all the equipment used during the course. I asked, already knowing the answer, why they didn't give us a lift in the transport. The answer from Alec was the now famous 'It's a question of mind over matter, kid. I don't mind and you don't matter, so effing well walk.' They then drove away. The walk back was about twelve miles. We all survived and felt a sense of achievement. That evening there was an end-of-course party which customarily turned into a beer fight, and we were all detained at Kiel for another day to clean up the bar area.

At this point I dwell on Alec Black. We were to meet again years later when I ran an Army diving team at Maidstone in Kent.

From this course, I learned that Army diving could be led by a guy who could maintain standards, efficiency and values, but did so with a great sense of humour. Sadly, this was rare.

Another great asset he had was never expecting anybody to do anything that he could not, or would not, do himself. I liked that, and have always tried to be the same. To explain in a small way what I mean, whilst we were at Hameln during the course, diving in the Weser, there was a bank robbery in the town, and whilst they caught the robbers, they never recovered the cash.

We were told that when the robbers took flight, they threw the money into the Weser from an iron bridge. The Weser is a navigable river, and at Hameln boasts the only set of double locks in Germany. Alongside the locks is a large weir, with the river cascading over it. The money was meant to be just on the upstream side of the weir. It was decided that we would enhance our fast water training by carrying out a lifeline search on top of the weir. Visually it looked very daunting. We were anchored in our boats onto the bank just twenty feet or so upstream of the weir. You could hardly hear or talk above the noise of the roaring water. Whilst we were preparing and sorting kit, I asked Alec who was to dive first. He said, 'I am', and he did just that. Once kitted up, he rolled backwards off the boat and stood up in four feet of water. Not even challenged. He took his mask off and spoke to the instructors 'This is it!!!! Get these effing divers in'. We dived successfully there, learned lessons and never found the money. More importantly, he would not let us dive it until he had proved the conditions himself.

At this time, as divers, we were paid per minute of time spent under water. We received half a crown (two shillings and sixpence) for 'test equipment' and the same for a splash dive, so each time we got into the water we earned five shillings, and for each minute we were under water we received one penny. These rates were doubled to two pennies per minute if you worked on sluices, wrecks or with explosives. From those days, I learned to keep an exact logbook record of all my dives (something I still do today).

Army Diving Supervisors/Instructors Course

In March 1968 I was selected to attend the Army Diving Supervisors Course No 9 at Marchwood. The course was again during a chilly time of the year, March to May, and little had changed at the school.

We did, however, have the luxury of different changing rooms, and were given a corrugated iron shed.

The course was good fun and included diving with some great and interesting equipment. Those who passed, became an Army Diving Supervisor (ADS) and were then qualified to supervise army divers within the constraints of the then military diving bible, the BR155. You also had to have the rank of corporal, which I had not yet reached (I had one rank to go). We were taught deep diving techniques and how to use and operate a re-compression chamber. We were taught and qualified in Standard

Diving equipment by a real expert called Mr Sam Stanley (more of Sam later).

We spread our wings and did a civil engineering project at Calshot on the Solent, which involved us planning and undertaking all aspects of the project.

Another fun day was a visit to the submarine escape tower at HMS Dolphin at Portsmouth. These were good times, and even though everything we did was assessed and marked, it was still fun. The 'Op Awkward' was, of course, still with us, as was the PT (physical training), but that was just a part of life.

A new skill that was taught to us was River Reconnaissance. The aim of this was to produce a profile of a river from bank to bank at all likely crossing sites. The cold war was at its height, and the army in those days relied heavily on an amphibious assault role to cross the main barrier rivers Rhine, Weser and Leine. Therefore, all army diving teams based in Germany had to be able to produce quickly and accurately the profile of the bottom of any river thought to be in the battle zone.

Later, you will see that the amphibious assault role in practice was not a success, but at that time the army had many vehicles that could wade, snorkel or swim. The amphibious role did go down fighting, literally, as will be seen later in the book.

Whilst I am still covering the ADS Course, I want to speak about the person who ran the re compression chamber and was responsible for instructing Standard Helmet diving.

He was a great character called Sam Stanley. Sam came to army diving after a successful career in the navy. He had reached

'Legend' status in the navy, and I have probably learned more about professional and practical diving from him than any other individual.

Many years later I met up with an ex naval guy, and we got talking about diving. This guy was a ships diver in the navy (the equivalent of ACAD). He said that in his time, the most revered of all the Clearance Diving instructors (CDs) in the navy was a guy called 'Diver Stanley'. I said 'Sam Stanley?' 'Yes', he replied. I said 'He trained me'. He instantly took me seriously as a diver.

Sam passed on his knowledge and skills, and I owe him a huge debt. Many years later I had cause to go back to the diving school for a diving convention. I took with me a gallon stone jar inside a wicker basket full of issue rum, which was found in the back of a store, and gave it to Sam. At an appointed time every day, Sam would take a tot of rum. Old habits die hard, and Sam was indeed a hard man. Well into his sixties, he would still dress in Standard helmet equipment and instruct the courses. When fully dressed the Standard diving equipment weighs one hundred and eighty seven pounds. He used to wear a tweed hat whilst diving in Standard. I can remember him demonstrating buoyancy control by jumping onto and over a metal workbench whilst underwater with all the deftness and skill of a ballet dancer. He was a master at his art.

After successfully completing the ADS course, including the exam, I was a brand new Army Diving Supervisor (ADS (Standard)). I was allowed to wear the ADS badge, which was a gold/yellow embroidered Standard diving helmet without the 'SW'. I was no longer a shark wrestler.

The equipment had progressed from Heinke MK V to mark VI. It was still a twin hosed regulator, which dumped all exhaust gases behind the divers head. It was a system preferred by photographers as they were not disturbed by exhaust gases flowing across their faces, whilst activating their cameras, particularly for close up work.

The one and only Mr. Sam Stanley, with his supper.

As we could now dive to much greater depths, we had the problem of 'squeeze', from the Avon dry suits. 'Squeeze' was the compression of air trapped in the drysuit and was quite a painful experience, if ignored. The air would contract in volume, due to the water pressure, and the suit would clamp the diver tightly, rendering him unable to move in severe cases. To alleviate this, the boffins gave us a small three and a half cubic foot cylinder, worn on a belt with loops around the waist. It fed air into the suit through a small hose, into a small brass threaded inlet on the front of the suit. It worked, but it was a clumsy, insecure and unsure method of suit inflation. The cylinder had to be charged to three thousand psi (one third more than our breathing cylinders). It required its own charging hose and HP outlet on the compressor, which meant that everywhere you went to dive you needed to take your own compressor (a four man lift). There was no way of knowing if it was full, partially filled or empty. We learned to crack open and close the valve quickly, and we used to gauge from the loudness of the crack whether there was sufficient HP air content for a dive, but you never really knew if that was the last crack of air. It also gave us another belt around our waist, which meant that for a while we had a knife belt (knives were later put onto the suit inflation belt), a weight belt and a harness belt. In short, it was a lash up and a great example of the person who designed it never ever had to wear it. We, however, soldiered on with it. Of course, you came unstuck if you ever dived with other nations' divers. There was no way to re-charge it.

I came across this problem years later when I went to Canada and attended the Canadian Combat Divers course in British Columbia (explained later on). The only way to overcome this was to make and adapt for myself a suit inflation system for the Avon dry suit, which ran from the low pressure outlet on my regulator. It was not really rocket science and similar systems had been in use by sub aqua divers for a couple of years. It was an example of how my dual underwater life, military and recreational diving proved to be beneficial to me. I had maintained a parallel interest in sport diving and dived as often as I could with my sport diving buddies. I consequently learned from them and kept abreast of new innovations and equipment.

Me dressed in standard helmet equipment during my supervisors course at Marchwood.

Whilst it is always a popular theme through life, with the benefit of hindsight, to laugh at or bemoan earlier times and the equipment used then (as I have just done about the suit inflation cylinder), it was about this time that someone found what looked like a mouldy old roll of rubberised canvas, at the back of an old store. Further investigation found that it had arms, legs and a torso. In the head hood was a small brass window, it was a 'Sladen Suit' which was worn by the famous 'charioteers', very brave divers from the generation before me. Of course, the man with all the answers was Sam Stanley. I tried the suit on, which was entered feet first through a trunk in the back. Then you wormed your way upright, put your head in the hood and looked and spoke through the hinged window. The entry/exit trunk was then rolled up and a cumbersome bronze screw clamp was tightened down over the roll, hoping to effect enough pressure to make the thing watertight. The exploits of the men who used these suits for real are explained in the book The Frogmen[1] by Waldron and Gleeson. The Sladen Suit was a fright. I realised, whilst in it, that if the suit had a bad tear or rip, then with the open flow system of air you could actually drown in the thing. The suit had the nickname of 'Clammy Death'. To all those brave 'charioteers', I salute you.

I returned to Germany and took up a new post in Hameln, a town I knew quite well. I was also promoted to the dizzy height of corporal. About this time, the divers pay changed. Instead of the 'penny-a-minutedived' system (explained earlier), we moved on to a scaled daily rate, but to qualify for the pay each diver must maintain a minimum amount of time under water each month.

I now ran the diving team for an engineer regiment in Hameln, as well as being a section commander. Both jobs kept me busy. Much of the diving training was done in the fast water of the River Weser. Carrying out underwater searches and producing river profiles played a major part in our lives.

We also used a local quarry for continuation training. Just before Christmas in 1968 the team kitted up and went to the quarry. It was iced over. We made an Eskimo-type fishing hole and dived on lifelines for training. It was my first experience in open water under ice (the tank at the diving school was obviously not open water). To say it was freezing would be stating the obvious, but it was. I had acquired a couple of Standard Helmet diving wrist seals, called 'greys' (that was their colour) and wore them over the Avon wrist seals to increase the efficiency of the seal. Whilst working under water, the tendons on your inner wrist would corrugate and allow water in to the suit. In the case of ice diving, it was like an icicle shooting up your arm and trickling down your armpit onto your torso. Within minutes you were

---

[1] T J Waldron & James Gleeson, *The Frogmen*, (Basingstoke, Hampshire, Macmillan), 1970.

numb and could easily reach a point where you could not take any more water in. This was called 'topping up'.

It was the last thing anyone would have wanted during a cold water dive. Not only was it inconvenient, but also dangerous, with a risk of hypothermia. So I wore the greys as a precaution against topping up. However, nothing in life is simple or easy. A side effect of the greys, because they were much tighter on your wrist, was to restrict the flow of blood to your hands, which made them numb. Then, of course, there was the danger of being unable to use your hands for simple safety practices, lifeline signals, ditch set routines and exiting the water. The compromise I came up with was to make my own greys from neoprene off cuts. They prevented water ingress whilst maintaining blood flow. This was another useful idea from my recreational diving life.

Stood on the frozen quarry deciding whereto place the entry/exit hole.

Hole dug and tested for size.

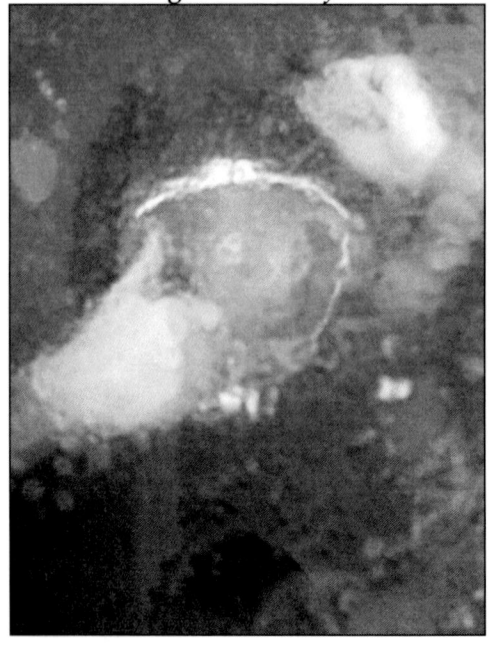

*I dive under the ice and appear under the team.
(note the lack of gloves and the grey wrist seals)*

I was attended by another diver during my dive under the ice, which is an essential safety requirement.

Combat Engineer Tractor Trials

By this time military boffins had invented a tracked bulldozer that could swim. It was called the Combat Engineer Tractor (CET), and they had brought a prototype to Germany for trials. It was painted yellow and therefore, not surprisingly, was called the Yellow Peril. It was an impressive machine and could, in fact, swim well and enter and exit on steep riverbanks. We were just there in case of emergency and we were not needed. We did, however, visit much of Germany and its waterways, and ended up in a small but lovely town called Witzenhausen on the River Werra. A few miles further downstream is the town of Hannoversch Muenden, where the River Werra joins the River Fulda and becomes the mighty Weser.

The CET went on into production and became one of the Army's most useful and versatile pieces of equipment. Apart from specific equipment such as floating bridges or boats it is now, I believe, the Army's only true amphibious vehicle. It was a fun task, working with the early CET and we visited many lovely parts of Germany.

The dive team and the scientists in front of the tractor.

The diving teams truck and administration tent where we slept.

The tractor under going trials in the River Werra.

Kiel, as Instructor

In October 1969 I was posted, as a diving instructor and supervisor, to the diving school at Kiel. It was, of course, a position I had dreamt of doing, and in a lovely part of the world. Kiel is fabulous. The diving school was a small team of supervisors/instructors, who ran the Combat Engineer Diving courses, which I had done previously, to train the army divers for their job in Germany. It comprised four Army Diving Supervisors (ADS), one Army Compressed Air Diver (ACAD, officer commanding), three drivers and a stores Non Commissioned Officer (NCO). It was a nine man self-contained team, located in a fantastic town on the Baltic Sea.

There was much history and maritime heritage at Kiel. It had a prominent role in both world wars, as a leading warship and submarine base. Similar to, say, Portsmouth. It now has both the main sailors' memorial at Laboe, and the U-Boat memorial at Moltenort. The former being a huge sandstone edifice in the shape of a submarine conning tower. Situated on the beach in front of the memorial is a World War II submarine mounted on concrete plinths through which visitors can walk. It is steeped in history, not only of the German navy, but was the sailing venue for both the 1936 and 1972 Olympic Games. It is a fascinating place, and to this day remains one of my favourite places in the world.

There were always plenty of interesting things to do including equipment maintenance and good varied diving.

I was in charge of the high-pressure portable air compressors. It was a job I actually did not want, but took on reluctantly. Engines and motors were not my forte, and I found myself responsible for four portable petrol driven air compressors; two Dunlop and two Siebe Gorman. During the normal routine they took a hammering. We anchored them to a trailer with turnbuckles, and they would travel with us everywhere, being shaken to death in transit or in use.

We overcame much of the problem caused by vibrations by sitting them on a truck tyre. They required high maintenance. The HP (high pressure) copper lines were all compression joints, which could come apart easily, and sometimes did whilst under pressure. They had a strict filter changing routine and the filter agents at the time were activated alumina, silica gel and copper lessing rings.

During my time at Kiel, I got to know compressors well, very well in fact, and the lessons learned during this time have held me in good stead for the rest of my diving life. I am now technically able to operate, service and maintain any compressor. Not that I wish to seem a big head here. It is just that since those days I have realised that if you want to achieve successful uninterrupted diving, then it is a fact of life that the whole success is dependant on the mechanical reliability of two pieces of equipment. These are the high-pressure (HP) compressor and the outboard motor (OBM). If they do not work, then nobody dives. This was all the incentive I needed to know and understand compressors.

The team at Kiel, when I arrived

*Me kitted up on the diving jetty,
(note the twin set, heinke mask and suit inflation cylinder.)*

Me dressed for a recreational dive in my self made neoprene suit.

Another tip here is that you can learn so many things by listening to the lessons and experiences of those before you. You will remember my writing about Alec Black and Sam Stanley. I learned much from them. I will now give you an example of when that philosophy did not work.

During the first part of my posting to Kiel, I was re-united with AA, my ex troop sergeant. He was now the Warrant Officer, and was in almost total charge of the unit. What a miserable experience for us all.

Sadly, there was no humour or hilarity, and his only method of achieving results was to threaten or make a woe-betide-you atmosphere, or to just shout louder. It became tedious, especially in such a small group. One of the other corporal instructors was a guy called Tom Downie. Tom deserves a mention. We met on the supervisors course. He was, at that time, in a parachute engineer unit. Tom is a streetwise Glaswegian and some 8 years older than I am. He would take great delight in setting me up with AA, and I would ship all of the flak, whilst he would walk away. It is quite safe to say, I spent much of my early time in Kiel in the shit, most of it dropped there by Tom. However things were to change.

A guy called John Briffitt replaced AA. Not that one should judge by looks, but Big John was the spitting image of a prize-fighter. 'So', I thought, 'I'll go from being continually bollocked here, to just getting beaten up!' However, things were not all they seemed. Big John had a delicate touch to his man management and, coming from a background of army transport, was excellent mechanically. He could see that, as the 'compressor man', I was not a square peg in a square hole. He asked me where

I had learned about them, and I said mostly self-taught. He said 'We'll put that right', and took it upon himself to show me. He proved to be the basis of what I know about air compressors nowadays and again, another good lesson learned. Additionally, and most importantly, some humour came back into the unit, and the sun came out. Another welcome development was the progression into enjoyable diving. John Briffitt was an excellent recreational diver. He had previously been on a posting to Hong Kong, where he had been a leading light in the sub aqua club. He was full of tales and experiences. He was also more streetwise than Tom Downie, so Tom stayed in his box like a good boy.

Chipping a hole through the sea ice.

Unlike freshwater ice, there is no clarity with sea water when frozen (note the diving pontoon which is usually free floating is now icebound)

Two divers tended by lifelines, begin their dive

The diving jetty in the bay during ice free times

The unit had a motor boat, which was called Taucher (German for diver), and was an ex British navy craft used to transfer sailors from ships to shore and vice versa. I believe they are called liberty boats. It had a canvas roof, an exposed wheelhouse and rows of benches, which could be folded away. It was never used. Big John saw this as a huge opportunity to get us out on to the high seas, and he did just that. During our periods of non-intensive activity, he would organise us to go off in the boat, sometimes for several days. It was a new and awesome experience for me, and was the grounding for my love of, and involvement in, diving expeditions.

Directly due north from Kiel is the Danish harbour town of Sonderborg, which we visited using Taucher. We also visited many other little fishing villages around the Baltic Sea. It was the start of a new set of adventures for me, which involved learning to dive at several new locations independently and self-contained. What you loaded on the boat had to support you for the duration.

No, it was not a Trans-Siberian adventure, but to work out the boat, fuel, air, food, clothing, diving kit, first aid, compressor, etc, etc, etc, took some attention to detail.

It was an adventure, and the beginning of my grounding for my expeditions. I look back now, and tick off some of the locations of the expeditions I have been on, to Africa, Central America, Falkland Islands, Australia, Borneo, Middle East, Norway, Orkney Islands, Outer Hebrides. All of them different, but the one thing they all have in common is, that it was all started by the influence of, and what I learned from John Briffitt. I enjoyed a tremendous sense of satisfaction and achievement through teamwork. It was a positive period in my diving life.

The only really big shadow in my life was that Big John had decided to give me the nickname 'Diddy'. Now, if you see yourself at age twenty two as a steel hard, underwater super hero who killed for a hobby, then 'Diddy' is not a nickname that you should have, giving people the impression of a Ken Dodd helper from Knotty Ash! However, as it originated from Big John, I heartily laughed it off !

John Briffit operating an assault boat alongside the awesome and imposing ruins of the submarine pens in Kiel harbour. The once very dominant and imposing ruins have now been removed.

This concrete blockhouse was tilted at a precarious angle from an explosion trying to destroy it. It was like a 'crazy house' in a fairground and some people felt nauseous whilst trying to walk through it.

Standing upright inside the bunker.'

To re-state the point about learning from one's forefathers. Sam Stanley, Alec Black, John Briffitt and others you will be told about as you read through the book, including my dear friend Douglas Bilbey, will show you that I did indeed stand on the shoulders of giants.

At this time the diving unit was tasked by divisional headquarters to provide safety cover during the amphibious assault phases of major exercises (I explained earlier that the army had major amphibious river crossings built into all exercises). The amphibious role took some selling to the lads on the ground. The main armoured personnel carrier (APC) was a sixteen-ton Behemoth, which drove on tracks. It was, and still is, the main personnel carrier in use. In those days it had an amphibious role when a rubber screen was lifted up around the upper edge of the vehicle. The screen was held rigidly in place by struts. The driver sat down in his normal seat in a cupola. The commander sat elevated, usually on a hatch cover, and relayed instructions through a headset to the driver. It required trust, confidence and experience.

Descending slowly down a bank at a precarious angle into a fast flowing river at night was not easy, particularly if either the commander or driver were non-swimmers. There was a critical point when, once in the water, the driver was instructed to give full gas. The vehicle would float and gain propulsion by the tracks and gain direction, port or starboard, from driving only one of the tracks. This caused the thing to swing around, sometimes turning full circles, as it was carried downstream. It could be done, but it needed all the aforementioned qualities, and was not often practised. Recovering sunken Armoured Personnel Carriers (APCs) was to become one of our main tasks. Not only was it essential to recover the weapons and the men's equipment, but there was no way you could leave a huge sixteen-ton metal obstruction in the middle of a navigation channel of a major river.

There was the usual crop of funnies. Very often the APC would misjudge the entry, and the unseeing driver would give it full gas too early. The APC would shoot head first into the black water, causing a huge bow wave to surge over the top of the screen and completely submerge the driver. Thinking he was drowning, he would abandon the controls and do an emergency exit, very often jumping off the back of the machine onto the bank. This would leave the commander, with headphones on, talking to himself, whilst on a sixteen-ton wreck floating helplessly with the current. On other occasions the screen would collapse under the force of the water surge, and the APC would drive slowly forward for up to twenty seconds, lying on the bottom, until the engine gave up.

There was another incident when, even after months/years of training in sending radio messages under duress, enemy fire, mine strikes etc., a young NCO in a Scottish unit was heard to scream 'I'm drooning, I'm drooning. Me nose has gan doon'. What ever happened to 'Mayday, mayday'? It was a role that the guys did not take to.

The driver could not wear a life jacket because its bulk prevented him getting out through the cupola. If he was a non swimmer, as many were in those days, you could hardly blame him for losing his cool when seemingly trapped in an armoured metal box, and under water. The same APCs are still in use today, but the rubber screens have now been removed.

Our dive boat in those days was known as the MK IV assault boat. It weighed four hundred pounds, was flat bottomed and had a false hull. It was made out of aluminium alloy. A rail all around the gun whale became a carrying and lifting handle, whilst lugging the boat out of water. The stern transom was flat and sometimes had a part cut away to accommodate short shaft OBMs. It was easily handled, could carry eight soldiers complete with kit, and was easily manoeuvred. The only downside was a high silhouette, which could be affected by side winds, but it did the job.

Sunken Armoured Personnel Carrier Recovery

If it was not a life-threatening situation, we could always recover vehicles at a time to suit us, and certainly in daylight. We nearly always knew where a wreck was by the large wave cascading over the vehicle.

At the beginning there were some hair-brained scenarios.

There was no way you could put a diver in upstream to approach a wreck. He would have been slammed against it and held there by the current, probably having his mask removed in the process. The problem was that, as soon as you moved your head ninety degrees in to the current, your mask either broke its seal and filled with water or was removed, such was the power of the current. There was no way you could be dropped downstream of the wreck and swim up to it. The probable outcome would have been collecting you at Bremerhaven in a bucket. Therefore, we had to descend vertically onto the wreck under control, ensuring that we could hang on securely as the waters raged around us. There was a problem with this. All the vehicles carried a huge camouflage net, which was placed loosely on top to be easily deployable to cover the vehicle when stationary. This net would now be wafting in the current. It would be just great if you slipped off the wreck due to the current and then sailed into the net. As any diver knows, the easiest way to die underwater is to swim into a net.

The next problem was attaching recovery slings to the recovery points and then attaching the other end of the sling to a recovery winch vehicle on the bank. There were recovery lugs situated front and back of the APC, so hopefully we could attach the slings on the downstream side and work in the lee, using the bulk of the wreck as protection from the current.

It didn't always work out like that. They often sank sideways on to the current, and peeping your little head round the corner to get to the lugs was like looking out of a train window at full speed. Dragging your body and sliding around to get to the recovery lugs to attach the sling with a big heavy shackle without losing your mask or being dragged off the wreck was an effort, believe me.

Another consideration was that the air supply from the regulator came via two corrugated hoses and, as I explained earlier, turning your head to the side was inadvisable. Keeping your head into the current sometimes caused the hoses to collapse, giving you very restricted breathing. We tried to overcome this by brazing a copper pipe to the mouthpiece in an arc following the natural path of the hoses. It was an improvement, but a lash-up, and also an unauthorised change. This, of course, meant that if a serious accident occurred we were all in the shit. Still, since when have we done as we were told?

Anyway, back to the wreck. What we had to do was devise a system that allowed the diver to descend vertically and safely onto the wreck. To do this we drove over the wreck in the assault boat and, by holding station against the current over the wreck, probed with a scaffolding pole into the wreck hoping to get it positioned in either the driver's or commander's cupola, all the way to the floor and wedged behind the seats. When done, the pole became rigid and as long as the pull on it was only exerted from the direction of the current, it remained rigid. Once it was positioned, we could attach the bow of the boat to it, and it then became a stable dive platform directly over the wreck. The diver would then descend on to the wreck, hand over hand on the scaffold pole (usually an effort to hang on, but that is where the non stop press-ups paid off !). When he reached the wreck, the first task would be to cut free any of the camouflage net from the wreck.

Another lesson was learned here. Nowadays there are specific cutters for nets, which are ideal, but in those days all we had were our knives, which certainly focussed us on our maintenance. Since then, I have always kept a well-honed knife. In fact I dive with two, one on each leg. However, then I dived with a knife that had not seen daylight for a while. When I pulled it out to work on a net it was embarrassing.

I am not saying it was blunt, but I could have ridden bare-arsed to China on it! Lesson learned. Having to re-surface to collect a decent knife cost me a round of beers — ouch!

Once the net peril had been removed, the next task was to recover all the valuables, which were usually located around the commanders cupola: binoculars, compass, and, of course, the machine gun. Also any other weapons from the section, including the driver's weapon and other valuables. Once done, we could concentrate on positioning the recovery strops.

It was hoped that either the front or back of the vehicle wreck was facing downstream and therefore in the lee of the current. If this were the case the diver would descend down the pole, taking with him a light line to which was attached the recovery sling. He would slowly drift backwards, grabbing handholds similar to a descending rock climber. He would ease himself over the rubber skirt and down the back/front of the vehicle. We always wore a lifeline attached to an attendant in the boat, but the lifeline would cause severe drag in the current and it was like being pulled along whilst walking. I used to gather three or four yards of lifeline and secure it with a slip knot to an anchor point so I did not have the drag, whilst I pulled the recovery sling towards me and quickly shackled the Y-shaped sling to the recovery lugs using shackles. If slick, the whole operation could take only a couple of minutes. I would then attach the light line to the end of the tail on the Y shape and signal 'five bells' (finished work). Having disconnected the anchored lifeline, I would then be signalled 'four pulls, two bells '(come up, hurry up). The ascent was the reverse of the descent, but harder, as it was against the current.

When the diver was safely back in the boat, we would pull up the end of the recovery sling on the light line and attach the main recovery winch cable. We divers would then get out of the way and hand over to the Army's recovery mechanics ('reccy mechs'), and they would winch the wreck out. When it was clear of the water, we would open the rear crew access door to release up to ten tons of water. Once it was safely up on the bank, it was job done. Sometimes the vehicle would throw off one or both of its tracks during the recovery. We would recover them later, again using the winch to drag them out.

We became quite adept at this type of recovery. If the wreck was sideways on, and the current was sweeping both the front and back of the vehicle, we would operate a two-phase recovery. The diver, clinging on for dear life, would rock climb around the windy corner and grab the recovery lug and haul a leg of the sling and shackle it onto. We would then stand clear, as the reccy mechs winched it in and swung the wreck around until the shackled side was out of the current. We would then dive and fix both sides of the Y sling.

To those, who, may think, that my habit of tying off my lifeline could prove dangerous, I agree. If I was pulled from the wreck by the current, there was every chance that I would be held spread-eagled in the current, downstream, with no means of signalling or surfacing. Although during this time I was incommunicado, it was usually for less than one minute that I was in danger of being dragged off the wreck. I did adapt a system where I used a carabineer to secure my lifeline and could still discern a signal through it, but the lifeline was continually shuddering in the current anyway. If there was an emergency recall of the diver, topside would initiate a loud underwater bang. It takes only a second to release the carabineer, and then you are free to 'surface immediately and state your condition'.

In addition to recovering APCs, there was much else to do. Any equipment dropped in the river could be recovered. Once we were awoken in the middle of the night and called out on a river crossing exercise. It was not swimming vehicles but a piece of equipment called a heavy ferry. Vehicles were supposed to drive on, stop, be ferried across and then drive off . Not exactly rocket science, but we arrived to see a chieftain tank sitting on the riverbed with the top of its turret and gun sticking out of the water. We were told that the tank commander had thought it was a bridge and just drove off the end. Things like that can happen when lads are exhausted. It was standard procedure for us to train at night-time during tactical exercises.

However, on this occasion we did not need to dive to attach the recovery slings, but could attach them by standing on the hull and reaching down, dressed only in surface swimming equipment.

Another recovery job was the propulsion pack from a heavy ferry. It had become dislodged whilst it was being built, and set off , spinning downstream with the current. It took with it a forlorn soldier who was doing his best to keep dry. The propulsion pack was very top heavy, and this individual, a non-swimmer, was trying desperately to keep it upright. However, every side he stood on lurched downwards, and he would then run to the upper side, only for that to sink too. To really help matters, the rest of his unit, some one hundred soldiers, were all running down both banks shouting advice. The safety tug could not approach because it would have capsized the pontoon on contact. It was quite hilarious to watch, and when it eventually turned turtle and sank, there was a large visible groan of dismay from the soldier's mates. I remember saying at the time how it seemed like great camaraderie to show compassion to their man. The guy next to me said 'Camaraderie my ass. Jonah there had the last packet of dry fags of the whole troop in his pocket'. Such is life. Life was about always being busy and being presented with the unexpected on an almost daily basis.

The Mk 5 assault boat being used as a safety boat on the river Weser.(Note the standby diver seated towards the stern)

The site of the sunken APC is clearly visible from the river bank. Note the radio aerial sticking above the water.

We have now attached the recovery strop and started to winch the vehicle out of the water. Here it is just breaking the surface'

Once the APC is clear of the water, the team secure any loose equipment and release the back doors under control, to release up to 10 tonnes of water from the inside.

It was now job done, (note the collapsed rubber skirt around the top of the vehicle)

Here you can see a good example of why the sunken military equipment had to be recovered from the river ASP, here, a piece of equipment called a 'Heavy Ferry' and a civilian tourist cruiser pass each other, there is no room for error.'

This photo of me was done by the Army recruiting agency and it was given to my local home town newspaper, the 'Bath Chronicle' and it was published with a small write up. It gives a good view of the twin x 38.5 cu ft steel cylinders and the heinke Mk 5 twin hose demand valve.

German Naval Facilities

The German Navy also had its diving centres nearby. Its main diving physiological centre was located at

Kronshagen in the suburbs of Kiel. The director of this facility at the time was German naval commander Dr. Karl Seeman who was very learned and eloquent. He gave lectures and presentations in fluent English. They had a superb RCC, and periodically we at the diving unit would go there for a deep dive to three hundred and twenty six feet (one hundred metres) on air, and decompress using pure oxygen. The RCC was state-of-the-art and it was always a privilege and a good experience to dive there. The next northerly coastal town of Eckernfoerde was the base for the German 'clearance diver' and 'combat diver' schools. We occasionally visited them to promote goodwill. They also had superb facilities.

Helicopter Jumps

One day we, the staff of the diving unit, were on such a visit. Our illustrious leader at the time was a young captain (ACAD) who had a lisp. We actually travelled up in his car and, upon arrival he went on board their headquarters ship to find out what we were going to do. I will never forget his happy little face as he came skipping back down the gangplank saying 'Geth thwat boyths, we´re doing helicopther jumpths!'

The helicopters concerned were old Wessex MKV, which we knew at the time were an absolute nightmare to jump from.

You had to sit at the door with your legs dangling loose. There was no skid to rest or step off from, so it was impossible to leave the aircraft in the optimal vertical position. The best you could do was just lurch forward, and then try to sort out a decent entry position by the time you hit the water. There were four of us, and about eight German lads all looking mean and sporting a crew cut, so there could be no backing out here. It was one of those 'for England and King Harry' occasions.

I was one who wanted to get this out of the way as soon as possible (as you will read later, I have a fear of heights), so I ensured that I was the second jumper to leave the aircraft. The guy in first place looked the part, but initially refused to jump and I could see why.

We were exceedingly high, and hovering with the rotor downdraft did not even affect the sea. He eventually went off and it seemed ages until he hit the water. Me next. Shoulder tap, then out I went just like a swastika in flight, and only just managed to sort out an entry position on impact. As you may know, when you hit the water in the wrong position, it is just like hitting concrete. I received a dead leg, but gave the OK signal and repositioned my right fin, which had come up to my knee, and started to swim to the jetty as instructed. I looked back at the others, swimming on my back in an almost sitting position, and was keen to watch them as they cart wheeled out. One of the last guys did such an exit and landing, you could have sold tickets to watch it. He creamed into the water with his face looking downwards and he was bent forward from the waist. He knocked himself out on impact and had to be rescued as he was lying face down. There was no great panic and, in the freezing water, he was soon back to consciousness, a bit like a boxer who had been dazed by a punch. It was our illustrious leader, poor sod, and he ended up with two such corking black eyes that he looked like a panda. I later discovered that the helicopter pilot had a bet with a destroyer captain that we would exit higher than the highest point of his ship, which explains the higher than usual jump. (The helicopter crew later told us that the height was twenty-seven metres.)

For weeks afterwards it was all the rage to mimic the 'Geth thwat boyths…' statement with the heavy lisp. Well, we thought it was funny.

By this time, we had leapt in technology to the Heinke MK VI regulator, and had carried out trials on a single hose system made by Spiro Technique. I had also been acquainted with a Draeger oxygen re-breather system at the German combat divers school. It gave me experience in a piece of new equipment.

Our old bible on diving, BR155, had been replaced by BR2806. They were both large family bible-size publications.

Around this time my posting at Kiel was coming to an end. I was posted to Tidworth, a large garrison near Salisbury plain. When I arrived there was little for me to do. The squadron I was joining had flown to the Caribbean for a military exercise and left me behind. As there was nothing useful for me to do, I was eventually stuck in the guardroom as a Regimental Police (RP). It was a mind numbing experience. Boredom and disenchantment crept in, and I bought myself out of the Army to become a civilian commercial diver.

1971-1973

Commercial Diving in Civilian Life

It was in January 1972 that my son Gary was born in Tidworth military hospital. A couple of months later, I was touting around the various commercial diving companies for work. In those days Great Yarmouth, Aberdeen and Southampton were the Meccas for diving and diver employment. Unwisely, we had no savings. I had married Anne, my childhood sweetheart, whom I met whilst at Dover. She had to live with her parents, whilst I hit the road. I phoned all the companies I knew, and had to pawn my radio to get petrol money to travel up to Great Yarmouth. En route my windscreen was smashed, and I had to go into debt to get it repaired. Not a good start. There were no jobs or work. However I recognized one of the lads coiling air hoses at one of the companies I visited, as one of my students from a course at Kiel. Most of the divers those days were ex-military.

The only lead I had was that a firm called Strongwork had a new contract to inspect bridges. I booked an interview in their Southampton office and drove down there the same day. I arrived and had my interview. Thankfully, I had an extensive engineering background and convinced them I was the man for the job.

The following Monday I was part of a three man team heading northwards. The contract was to inspect one hundred and twenty British Rail bridges in the northeast region.

Now, to dispel any myths about how well paid divers were, let me explain. There were two sides to the industry, onshore and off shore. Onshore were mainly civil engineering tasks in and around the coastal area and inland. It meant canals, rivers and harbours; sluices, sewers and the like; long hours, hard work and filthy water. Off shore was generally an oil or gas platform, either semi-submersible or jack-up types, located off shore. The diving was usually deeper, the water much clearer and conditions of work better. Meals and accommodation were provided. It was usually shift work, with say, two or three weeks on and one week off. It was an easier life apart from one thing. It was a prison.

There was one group of divers who worked on semi-submersible rigs, and therefore in deeper water, who spent their time in a pressurised chamber at the equivalent of the working depth of the platform (or rig). These divers were kept under constant pressure and were sent down to work in a diving bell. They were, therefore, transferred under pressure (TUP), did their task, and returned to the diving bell. Then they were transferred back to the main chamber. These lads were known as saturation divers or SAT divers. SAT diving was where the big money was, but it was less than two percent of the diving industry. The main advantage with SAT diving was that it eliminated the need for the divers to do decompression whilst in the water. The rig could not operate whilst divers were in the water. If divers had to do lengthy in-water decompression, it would cost the owner company a lot of money. By using an SAT diving system, the need for in-water decompression was eliminated.

The diving bell of my new civilian employers, 'Strongwork'.

I am being dressed in 'standard diving dress' by a couple of ex – navy buddies, also taught by Sam Stanley, it's a small world.'

My turn to repay the favour as I attend another standard diver'.

If you wished to become an SAT diver, it was mostly luck and being in the right place at the right time. During those days, there was no measured level of diving competence, and the industry employed a whole assortment of divers with a variety of standards and nationalities. There were some whose only claim to fame was to be able to blag off during an interview and impress. It was a bit like asking a man 'How good are you at sex?' Well, we all think we are the greatest. However, ask our partners, and you will probably get a much different answer. Ask a lad on a diving job interview 'How good a diver are you?' The response will be, 'The best'. If you were able to ask Neptune the same question, he would probably fall from his throne laughing.

So, in those days the answer was to steadily build yourself a reputation.

Having qualifications from a trusted source like the military was a good benchmark. Those days had no health and safety overview for the protection of the workers in any industry, so there were some really hairy practices, and stories to make your hair curl.

Inspection of One Hundred and Twenty British Rail Bridges

Anyway, back to the northeast contract. The job was to inspect and check the foundations of 120 British Rail bridges, in and on the water. The area ranged from the large multi-arched railway bridge at Berwick down to Goole and Selby. We did the big bridges on the Tyne at Newcastle. We lived in bed and breakfast accommodation around the area. It was my first time in that part of the world. I got to see a lot of new scenery, and met lots of interesting people. We produced a photographic report for each bridge and, where necessary, accurate drawings of any findings. We did a total of two hundred bridges, which meant two hundred reports. Job done. It was back to Southampton.

They were a busy few weeks, and the living was not good. Eating rubbish and sleeping in a variety of locations were wearying. In addition, although I was being paid enough to live on and support Annie and Gary, we were unable to build up any savings. Annie lived with her parents in Chatham and this was not a home. Also, I had to pay for accommodation in Southampton. This meant that all my wages were being used up in a very expensive lifestyle, on bed and breakfast, accommodation and travel costs.

Contract to Repair the Cracks in the Reactor Transfer Tunnel, Winfrith Nuclear Reactor, Dorset

The next contract was at Lulworth in Dorset, a very beautiful part of the world and an area that remains one of my favourite places to this day. At Winfrith, just outside Lulworth, is a nuclear reactor. The reactor was a state-of-the-art construction when new, but was now aged. Now, quoting the boffins' technical jargon as well as I can remember, deep in the bowels of the reactor are two large ponds. One of the ponds is a storage facility for the nuclear fuel rods, and the other pond is the reactor face. A transfer tunnel, perhaps thirty metres long, connects the two. Although concrete, the walls were coated with white plastic and illuminated with neon lights. The water was crystal clear, so it was like diving in gin. The rods would be transferred through the tunnel via a stainless steel rail construction, where the rods would dangle below a cradle with wheels. The cradle would then be impelled along the rails. I do not know how, but for certain it was not driven like a car!

On each side of the transfer tunnel were two separate ponds of water. They were used as cooling ponds, and water would be drawn from them and pumped/piped around the reactor as a coolant to all the places that needed it (stating the bleeding obvious). Now, when something goes wrong or off balance, it causes the reactor building to shake and then rock. It is a bit like a washing machine on its spin cycle. When it has an uneven load, it starts to jump about.

Those of us in the know call this rocking/shaking from imbalance a 'trip'. Apparently there are two types of trip; an X and a Y. An X trip is where there are minor tremors to the building, and a Y trip is where you send the bulldozers in later to flatten the building. As a result of a couple of X trips, cracks had appeared in the wall of the transfer tunnel. The fear was that contaminated water was seeping in to the cooling ponds, and then being pumped around the whole reactor building. Apparently, this is not recommended. To discover whether or not the cracks were connecting between the tunnel and cooling ponds, a head of water was pumped into the tunnel making it higher/deeper than the level in the cooling ponds.

One of our special scientific divers then dived in to the transfer tunnel with specialist equipment to ascertain if there was any flow into the cracks. The chief scientific diver was me, and the specialist scientific equipment was a squeegy washing up liquid bottle full of red dye. By releasing a squirt of red dye down the crack and watching, you could easily see that the dye disappeared into the crack. So, it was bad news for the UKAEA (United Kingdom Atomic Energy Authority). We had to make the crack watertight.

All the diving equipment used ended up contaminated and had to be left inside the reactor. It is, I believe, still on a concrete platform above the cooling ponds. Of course, we could not use ordinary scuba equipment because we could not take the cylinders back out to recharge them when empty, so we rigged up surface demand equipment with an air source outside the building. The airline passed through all the airlocks into the contaminated area and into the second stage of the diver's regulator. The diver wore a bale out cylinder in case of system failure of the surface demand.

The plan was to clamp a patch of industrial rubber and stainless steel over the length of the cracks on both the tunnel and the pond. Once fixed, epoxy resin would be pumped under the rubber, causing it to expand and bubble under pressure, and force the epoxy into the cracks. We used air tools to secure rawlbolts, to which the rubber and then the stainless steel frame was bolted. It took a few weeks to complete the job, and to prove that it worked.

On the domestic front things were tense. I had hired a mobile home in Southampton and Annie moved down. It was better than nothing. Two days later we drove down to Lulworth where we had booked a bed and breakfast. We arrived exhausted, only to be met by the greedy old witch who owned it. She told us no babies were allowed. The mobile home, for which I had paid three months rent but only used for one night, was never used again. When I asked the owner, the daughter of a rather wealthy family, and her Dutch boyfriend for a refund, explaining that my company had sent me away, I was told no chance. So, in Lulworth, I eventually hired a holiday caravan, and that gave us a settled few weeks. The weather was nice, and I went home every night. The beaches and coastal scenery there were beautiful.

'Reactor storage ponds, as you can see, you would never ever dive in clearer water, it was like diving in 'Gin'.

Strongwork, my employers, had a couple of old navy divers there as supervisors: Tom Norman and Happy Day. They were good guys and we were on the same wavelength. However, we did not work a lot together, as they were mainly used off shore. I noticed their signatures in my logbook from the times we worked together. If you ever read this book fellas, greetings to you, and do not ever forget that army divers do it deeper and better!!!

I digress.

Since the days of being paid a penny a minute, I had the habit of meticulously keeping a logbook, which I still do to this day. I use photos, charts, and any other useful available data, and stick them in the logbooks for future reference. You never know if or when you might be back at the same place, and your old logbooks then become a good point of reference, instead of working totally blind.

At the time, the logbooks we had to use as commercial divers were provided by CIRIA (Construction Industry Research and Information Association). It was an A3 size publication, and it was meant to be an effort to consolidate all the various diving factions under one umbrella, and was an accountable document. Nothing new to me, as military logbooks were always accountable.

It was not the first time my company had been contracted to dive in the Winfrith reactor. A couple of years earlier they had worked inside the contaminated area. This was reached via a series of airlocks and lead brick barriers, into a changing room where you were issued coveralls and socks and shoes. Street clothes did not pass beyond this point. Additionally, there were stores and tools in the contaminated area, which never left because they may have some contamination.

Therefore, when we needed tools we used theirs. When we needed specialist tools they were purchased, used, and then left inside 'contaminated'.

One day, whilst working in the tunnel, I dropped a spanner. It was so bright I almost needed sunglasses. No big deal, the depth was only twenty-five feet. So I thought I would just nip down and pick it up. Usually, if working suspended in nil visibility or in deep water, you would put a lanyard on the tool and attach it to your wrist. I noticed though, when it landed, that there was a little puff of dust. I picked it up and finished the job. When I tried to exit the complex, having showered and changed my clothes, my hands activated the radiac survey meter. The levels were not anywhere near fatal, but I had to scrub until they were passable. It was lunchtime, and the rest of the team, who were dying to get to the pub, were really impressed. In the end they made me wear a pair of latex gloves. There I was in the pub, drinking a pint wearing latex gloves, and getting some serious sideways looks. In the van on the way back my comrades said that, whilst I was in the toilet, the locals asked why I was wearing rubber gloves. They said that I was a gynaecologist who had just popped out for some lunch. Thanks mates!!!

When we went back to the reactor, I went to the decontamination laboratory where they removed the gloves and tested my hands. They again showed contamination.

Up to this point I had been using a special green gel, which they gave me to scrub my hands. The boffin then said to me, 'This calls for extreme measures, but do not tell anyone about this' (so you have not heard it from me, right!). He reached under the sink and gave me a tube of Vim, ordinary household Vim. I scrubbed with that, and my hands were clear. Thank goodness for modern science.

When the company last had worked there, they used the standard hard hat helmet equipment, which, although clumsy, fitted the criteria for providing a self-contained surface demand equipment. They had to leave it in there afterwards, as it was contaminated. Those copper and brass helmets are much sought after nowadays. When we were working there, there was no sign of it. One of the other workers had obviously smuggled it out and kept it as an ornament. I can imagine that he is confused as to why it glows in the dark.

So, enough of Winfrith, job done.

Replacement of the Lock Gate Sill, Penzance, Cornwall

Onwards, onwards. The next contract was at Penzance in Cornwall, which for me meant back to my heritage. We loaded up our little car and set off . We called at a farmhouse off the A30, a few miles out of Penzance, and asked if there was any room at the inn. They had a caravan in the farmyard, which they hired to us. It became home for almost two months. I commuted every day to the job. The rest of the divers were accommodated in the beautiful town of St. Ives. The company had a strong recent association with the area, as the previous year they had repaired a breach by the sea into the tin mine at Lelant, a short distance up the coast from St.Ives (very often, in Cornwall, mining tunnels project out under the sea).

It was summer, the weather was fine and the caravan became a good but isolated home. Annie could not drive in those days, so it was difficult for her to get to the shops.

There was no late opening back then, so by the time I arrived home with the car everywhere was shut.

The job was thus. Penzance had an inner harbour, which was accessed through some lock gates. The idea being that, whenever it was high tide, the gates could be closed allowing all the craft in the harbour to remain afloat. The sill along the base of the gates had eroded and was no longer watertight. Therefore, during the course of the tide ebbing, the water in the inner harbour would gradually flow out under the lock gates until the inner harbour was empty. Our job was to replace the sill. The plan was to remove the old sill and dig a trench to accommodate the new sill. The new sill comprised a series of pre-cast reinforced concrete blocks with a dovetail at each end. This, when positioned, would jigsaw together and form a seal. The whole construction would then be consolidated by grout, pumped in to the trench to fill any remaining gaps. We used a surface demand system, and operated out of a garden shed that we had erected on the pier wall above the job. It also became our changing room and lock up store. The daily routine was that I dived all morning and the other diver dived in the afternoon. It was relatively shallow water so there were no problems with decompression. Using a compressed air road breaker, we broke up the old sill and rolled the bits into metal crates. When full, we lifted the crates out using a dockside crane. This work took its toll on my suit. I was using an Avon dry suit, and wrestling with large lumps of concrete underwater was putting a lot of holes into it. Now, when you are underwater for between three and four hours daily, you do not want to be wet (and then cold), so it became a daily task to repair my suit. I ran out of patches and started to use bits of seam tape. Even small damage, the size of a pinhole, would top you up after an hour or so. Of course the suit, made of rubberised canvas, had to be washed in fresh water and dried before it could be repaired. It was almost back to the days of my basic course at Marchwood.

Once the old sill had been removed, we had a trench along the gate line. The new sill was much deeper than the old one, so we had to excavate a deeper trench. As I did the morning dives, I would usually meet up with a conger eel which lived in the wall behind the lock gates. The trench had to be cut from rock strata called Blue Elvin, which, I was told by an old tin miner, was harder than granite. The heavy breaker had two digging attachments, a spade and a spike, and we would use either depending on the rock. If we made a crack in the Blue Elvin, we would then chase along it with the breaker. At times the breaker would wedge itself in a crack and it would take up to 50 minutes of non stop breaking, as the hammer was wedged in the vertical position. The exhaust air from the breaker would spiral upwards just past my head. The conger eel found these exhaust bubbles quite fascinating and would swim into them and turn circles coming back in and out of them. During such long boring stints on the breaker, I would remove one of my greys and slide it over the handle grip and operating lever, so that it operated itself and did not need me. I left it operating and had a swim around to see what there was to see, periodically popping back to see how things were going.

When the trench was almost done we made a template profile of the new sill out of timber and moved it along the trench, marking high spots with underwater chalk to enable the breaker operator to fine tune the trench. We did not want to cut more Blue Elvin than was absolutely necessary. We also encountered old cast iron hinges from a previous gate. They were huge and had to be removed.

The lock gates to the inner harbour at Penzance, which we had come to replace the sill.

The dive work site from the surface at Penzance.

A section of the old sill having been broken by heavy breaker and lifted by hand into metal baskets and lifted out onto the quay by the dockside derrick. (The manhandling caused severe wear to my Avon drysuit.)

A ship passing through the lockgates.

Using buoyancy to position the new concrete slabs

*The site at Penzance.
Note the changing and equipment huts*

The best way to do this was with flexible thermal lance equipment called Keri Cable (named after the inventor's daughter). I used approximately two hundred and fifty feet of lance and the hinges were burnt off.

One problem with cutting cast iron is that, if the operator is inexperienced, the molten metal forms a 'pond'. If there is no drainaway, the thermal lance gets fed into the molten pond and the plastic coating melts away, allowing the oxygen to escape early and not reach the flame. The lance then extinguishes itself, but it is not like a match or candle going out. It gives off an explosion like a detonator. So avoid that if you can, girls and boys.

I later hired a holiday house in St. Ives for Annie, Gary and myself. It was a lovely cottage and Gary took his first steps there. Literally, a big step in anyone's life. St. Ives is a lovely town and every time we revisit, we take a look at the holiday cottage and all the old haunts.

There was a downside during the Penzance contract. For whatever reason, I developed boils in both of my ears. Whether they were brought on by the concussion effect of the breaker being amplified due to operating in a relatively confined space, dirty water or continual changes in pressure, I do not know, but I have never experienced pain like it. I could not touch my head or lay it on a pillow. It was awful, and of course I was still doing my daily shift underwater. There was no question of going sick, as we were under time pressure to get the job done. The Blue Elvin had slowed us down, as it was so difficult to trench through it. I went almost three weeks without sleep, just grabbing catnaps in a chair. I eventually had to go to the Accident and Emergency at the local hospital, and was immediately sent to an ENT specialist.

He confirmed the presence of boils in both ears and an infection. He gave me some painkillers and antibiotics, and that night, without going into too much detail, they burst. Although it was very painful, the relief of a different type of pain was quite exquisite. That night, after some three weeks of hell, I fell asleep like a baby. At twenty past two in the morning, during my first decent night's sleep for several weeks, I was awoken by very loud bangs in the sky. It was a series of explosive rockets calling out the lifeboat crew to muster stations. Ain't that the way it goes?

We bid farewell to Cornwall, again job done, and returned to Southampton. Annie went home again, to her parents.

There were no waiting contracts, but there was a lot maintenance to do on the kit. I mentioned earlier that I was a carpenter and joiner.

When the managing director, a very approachable and affable ex navy guy called Harry Wardle, discovered this there suddenly appeared a whole raft of jobs to do at his house, which I did. Harry was a likeable man and proved very understanding to me later on.

Construction and Anchoring of Pipeline, Holyhead, North Wales

Christmas came and went, and our domestic plight was unchanged. We did not have enough savings to buy our own house. Any spare money was taken by living in temporary accommodation. It was very frustrating. In the New Year I set off again to Southampton. The next contract would be in Holyhead on Anglesey, or more precisely, Treaddur Bay. Strongwork had, the previous year, constructed a sewage pipeline out to sea. The winter gales had arrived and they were unable to finish the task completely, so up we went. The outstanding task was to anchor the length and end of the pipeline, against the fierce currents that zip around those parts.

We anchored the pipeline at intervals along its length using concrete saddles, but there was still a danger from scour erosion caused by the strong currents. The job was quite basic, to bag up around the saddles and end of the pipeline to prevent scour. To achieve this, we used sandbags filled with a dry concrete mix. I have to say, I saw the biggest ever crab at the end of the pipeline with its claws and small pincers in the effluent being discharged. It must have been like a fast food restaurant for him. I then heard that Gary was very ill. The job had been completed at Anglesey, so the supervisor Happy Day sent me back.

A diver working on the pipeline

Annie was distraught. Gary had contracted pneumonia. She was breaking her heart. The insecurity of no place of our own, the fraught living with parents and separation was taking its toll. Gary's illness was the final straw. It was a dilemma, and at the back of my mind was a fairly easy solution. After a few enquiries, and the promise of a house immediately, I decided to rejoin the Army.

Back at the Strongwork depot in Southampton, I was summoned to see Harry Wardle, the managing director. He said he had heard about my dilemma and had been told I was thinking of re-enlisting and asked why. He made it plain that he did not want to see me go, and offered me a quick fix financially. He said that he would give me a job in the Middle East on a platform (rig), which paid well and would allow me to save enough to put a deposit on a house. It was a great offer, as the job was much sought after by other divers, but I explained that I had promised Annie and committed myself to the Army. He understood, shook my hand and wished me well.

1973-1979

Back into Uniform

During my previous spell in the Army I had been a corps canoeist, specialising in a long distance race called the Devizes to Westminster. The corps team was assembling at Maidstone and I went there on posting. Within two weeks I had moved in to an Army house called a quarter. The unit did not have a diving supervisor and I slotted in to that role. I got my rank of corporal back, but lost all seniority and started from scratch again. The unit was a strategic reserve regiment and could be called upon at short notice to deploy anywhere in the world. At the time I re-joined, army divers were constructing a concrete mole and slipway in Cyprus where things were not going well. Most of the work required underwater skills in concreting and construction, and the project was beset with problems.

As I said earlier, my unit was ready to fly anywhere at short notice, and the diving team was put on standby. The unit that was currently in charge out there was none other that the Army diving school. That hallowed ivory tower of instructors! They heard that we were meant to deploy out there and I was the supervisor. My unit was immediately informed that, as far as they were concerned, Liddicoat was an out of date diver and would not be a supervisor until he re-qualified. Therefore, some of my unit's divers were taken and I stayed behind, supposedly without any qualifications (the task out there was changed in format and they ended up with a much lesser construction than originally planned).

Re-Qualification in the Army

In order to re-qualify I had to go down to Marchwood and re-sit the exams. As there had been some changes with equipment during my time out of the Army, I made a couple of mistakes with the new exams. The exam papers were taken away to be marked by an old friend of mine, Geordie Thomson, who realised that I would drop marks needlessly. Although he could not make it himself, he asked a colleague to come down earlier in the morning and give me a re-sit of the exam questions I had messed up. It was camaraderie of the highest order.

I passed the exam but they still insisted on a practical test. For this I was put in charge of the diving display for the army show at Chatham. It involved a portable diving tank with a glass front like an aquarium some twenty feet by fifteen feet by ten feet, filled with water. We were to display divers in various forms of dress in the dive tank. They would perform simple tasks in front of the crowd. Steve Hambrook, the Sergeant Major Instructor (SMI) at the time, oversaw me.

The diving display tank, which was a centre point of Army Displays and proved very popular with the visitors

I think it was the first time I had worked for him. He left me alone and did not micro manage. He asked me to write an essay on army diving as part of the test. Upon reading it he told me that he agreed with me about many of the ideas in my script.

On the fourteenth of June I was certified by Steve to continue supervising. A word on Steve, who was a prominent character in army diving. Whilst in bomb disposal he was called out to defuse a huge wartime bomb. The bomb was in the middle of a built up area and for this action he was awarded the George Cross. Later in his career, whilst mine clearing in the Falklands, he lost a leg but continues his career wearing a prosthetic. In all of my dealings with Steve I always got a good return and a helpful attitude, and you have to say well done to his achievements.

In the unit of 'fly anywhere instantly' I sat on my packed suitcase for some five weeks flicking through my passport. Keeping myself sharpened and honed to a fine edge bore fruit and I was sent, war ready, to Aldershot! I was to supervise the diving tank for the army demonstration held at the Rushmore arena. It was a similar scenario to the display mentioned previously, but in front of a much larger crowd.

We were now trialling new diving equipment called Swimmers Air Breathing Apparatus (SABA), which the Navy were already using. However, the army continued using the Heinke MK VI for a few more years.

In 1974 I bumped in to an old friend. I had a phone call from Alec Black who had now left the army and was running his own parachute school at Port Lympre in Kent. He was planning an open day and free fall demonstration, and wanted to parachute into the sea. He asked me to provide safety cover and recovery of parachutists from the sea on the day. We were only too pleased to help, and there was the promise of a super barbecue in the evening with a suckling pig.

We went down to Dungeness where the demonstration was due to take place, but the winds were too high and the jump was cancelled. As we were there we dived in the bay. It was good to get a dive in the sea. That evening was uneventful. The barbecue seemed full of posh and influential people, so the diving team got undressed behind a wall and streaked through the multitudes. It went down a treat, and when we got back to the wall where our clothes rested, one guy's underpants had been eaten by a pig (the streak was the new craze in those days).

It was the last time I saw Alec. Some time later he was killed in a plane crash whilst piloting his own aircraft. Eighteen years later, when I was running a survival school in Kent, one of my team of instructors was a guy called Reg, a poacher. He saw an old photo of Alex and recognised him as his parachute instructor. Reg and I maintain good contact, and he thinks very highly of Alec Black, as I do. Rest in peace Alec. It is a small world.

A Struggle to Promote the Cause of Diving

It was always a struggle in the Army to convince the hierarchy about the usefulness of having divers on their books. Diving was still a specialist qualification and, apart from those being posted to either of the diving schools, all divers had other jobs to do within the unit. In many cases, because the divers were generally fit and ambitious (and in my case handsome, virile and modest!), they filled key alternative roles. Therefore, for the head of a unit to lose people in key positions to diving training without visible benefit was, at times, difficult to accept. I recognised this and knew that the more the diving team could fulfil a useful role to benefit the many instead of the few, the more we would be appreciated. It would be far better than being looked upon as a bunch of prima donnas who received very high specialist pay (up to five pounds per day by now) and often skipped normal training to do diving. One of the ways we tried was to offer sub aqua training to the common man in the unit. The Army gives adventure training a high priority. It sees and understands the benefits to teams and individuals. The term encompasses trekking, rock-climbing, canoeing, mountaineering, and other such pursuits. If you can add diving to that list it is generally appreciated, particularly when in an exotic location. I maintained a parallel life with my diving, and most weekends I took part in recreational diving, later known as sub aqua.

Sub aqua attracted a lot of lads who wanted to dive, but did not want the rigours of doing a military course. Many of the theory lectures in both were identical. The effects of water pressure are the same, regardless of the equipment being worn. There were just some differences in the equipment and communication underwater. The subaqua code has a series of basic hand signals, whereas its military and commercial counterparts do not expect to dive in water clear enough to see another diver. I used to take some stick from the army-only divers for my participation in subaqua. At one army diving convention in the 1970s almost every speaker poked fun at me and I had to take the flak.

The man in charge of all army diving is called the Superintendent of Diving, with the rather appropriate initials SOD. Even he joined in, and in the main it was light-hearted banter. They gave me the nickname Scoobie Doo (after the term scuba). Like all nicknames I accepted it and was quietly pleased that Diddy had fallen from the perch.

Scotland, Part: Adventure Training Teaching the Army

In 1974 the unit organised an adventurous training exercise in Scotland. The equipment travelled up by road and we went up by rail. The place was called Plockton, on the shore of Loch Carron. We were accommodated in the old disused schoolhouse in the village. If you have never dived in Scotland, I can only tell you that it is breathtaking. After this episode there were many other diving occasions all over Scotland. The diving, scenery and beaches are as stunning as any I have seen in my life. Only one thing is lacking, temperature!

I used such exercises to carry out sub-aqua training. In those days they were called aptitude tests (nowadays they are called try-dives or suck and see).

I converted as much of the army kit for sub-aqua use as I could. The only additional things needed were half masks and snorkels.

A huge improvement for army kit at this time was the issue of open backed jet fins. Previously we had the most useless piece of equipment it has ever been my misfortune to use. A pair of fins which, when viewed from above, copied the outline of a fish tail. Another great example of he who designs it is not going to wear it! They had the effect of making people swim in circles. The strap was not adjustable and usually so tight that it resembled a cheese cutter through the back of your heel.

Anyway, I digressed, back to Plockton. The only watering hole in Plockton was called Seaforth Hotel. It was an excellent example of a village pub and seaside restaurant combined. The view from it was over the loch and it was breathtaking. We did all our aptitude tests around the stone slipway and the state of the tide would depend on how far down the slipway we went. However, all the activity was done in full view of the locals, who often formed a crowd of spectators. The word spread that we were doing basic diving training at the jetty. Occasionally we would get a request from a local to have a go, and of course usually there was no problem with that. It went some way to integrate us. We were, after all, guests there. One of those who showed much interest was the barman from the hotel; a guy called Norry Ramsay.

Some people find it very difficult to ask outright, so we got lots of 'Wow! That must be great', 'I'd love to try it' and 'What do I have to do to get a go?' Simple, just ask. Some people who did the aptitude dive were naturals at it, and you could see in a heartbeat those who took to it and those who did not, but they all got the same chance.

The best way to do it, particularly if there are a lot of people, is to give one talk explaining mask fitting, pressure effects, hand signals and clearing ears. They should then go through a conveyor belt of trained divers. At the end they come out kitted up and ready for the water. They are then handed over to the in-water supervisor and begin the dive. Almost all the success of the venture is dependent on a well fitting mask. If their mask is leaking, water gets in their eyes and up their nose and they think they are drowning. Their immediate action is to strike for the surface. In doing so they would generally manage to knee you in the groin and rip off your mask. You would be in hot pursuit of them, whilst trying to reposition and clear your own mask. The depth of water was never great enough to be a problem, a maximum of three to four metres. The really good natural testers could later be guided to join a local subaqua club if they wanted to pursue the sport. With Norry Ramsay it was slightly different. Due to his working hours in the hotel he could not make the usual test times, so I tested him on a Saturday morning and he loved it. That evening he was still full of it, and when we left Plockton he gave me a bottle of twelve-year-old Glenfiddich whiskey as a thank you.

Apart from the novice testing, the team took the opportunity to do some deep diving in the loch. We were rewarded with some fantastic scallops, which are still my favourite seafood. I froze some and took them back to share with

Annie and Gary. When divers are spotted in such locations, it is very common for the local fishermen, sailors or just general boat users to ask them to recover whatever they have lost or dropped overboard, or to check on the state of their hull or propeller.

A real plus was a visit by the commanding officer who, in his youth, had done the Army diving course. He wanted some scallops so, during his two-day visit, we managed just that. He accompanied me on a dive to get some scallops. It had been a while since he had dived so I was able to keep an eye on him.

During the descent he had trouble clearing his ears. We were on a shot line and I could see the problem. He was wearing neoprene mittens that were too big for him, so he could not pinch his nose properly. I went up and, using my thumbs, one on each side, pressed his nostrils together. He was able to clear his ears.

The dive was good and we collected a bag of scallops. Later that day in a quiet moment he said to me 'Thanks for that Liddicoat. It was just the thing'. I said 'That's ok sir, anytime. It made me a load of money'. 'How come?' he asked. I told him that, at breakfast, I had bet the rest of the team that before the day was out I would have my thumbs stuck up the CO's nose. Thankfully he saw the funny side (and I only got fourteen days in gaol!). He was impressed with the tests on the lads, and he left us very much on side towards the diving team in his unit. He was to prove a great ally later on.

Helicopter Recovery, off Portland Bill

After Plockton I went back to my main job, that of Section Commander. As such I found myself down in Weymouth at a place called Wyke Regis, which has a small tidal river inside a long bank of pebbles called Chesil Beach. Although tidal, it was a good facility for fast water training, bridging and ferrying, and the Army has a large training camp facility there. I had only been there a couple of days when we were called out as an emergency diving team.

A Wessex Mark V helicopter on anti-submarine training had crashed and sunk in the sea between Chesil Beach and Portland Bill. We were going to work alongside a navy team to find and recover it. Thankfully, all of the crew had survived.

To aid in the recovery we had a large merchant navy ship called Kinbrace, with a huge hoist on its bow. We went on board and met the navy boys. The wreckage had been located and we had to secure the lifting slings around the lifting point. This was explained to us as the bit where the rotor blades (now missing) met. It was a cruciform of iron, which would revolve around and control the speed of the rotor blades. On the side window of the bridge on Kinbrace there was a line of hand painted silhouettes of the various objects the ship had salvaged, similar to wartime aeroplanes. There were a couple of aeroplanes, some boats and another helicopter. I decided that they would not need any advice from me.

I was asked to dive and saw, for the first time ever in British waters, the dorsal fin of a porbeagle shark swimming around the inflatable. The navy guys threw underwater bangs around it, and it disappeared. The shark was quite close (one hundred and fifty yards) to the shore, and five metres from the boat. It was well before the film Jaws, so there was no accompanying oboe music!

I kitted up in the Gemini inflatable boat and rolled over the side. I said that I would like to dive down first to look at how the helicopter was lying. I did not want to lug a big recovery strop around, only to discover I was nowhere near where I wanted to be. You may remember that the Wessex Mark V was the same aircraft I jumped from at Eckernfoerde. Therefore, I knew my way around it quite well. I found and memorised my wa to the slinging point. Thankfully it was readily accessible, so the job would be a cinch. I surfaced, collected the strop and dived down and connected it. I signalled five bells, finished work job done, surfaced, and got back into the Gemini boat. They started to winch it out. It looked huge. Once it was secured, the good ship Kinbrace slipped anchor and sailed off around Portland Bill to the navy dockyard. The Army guys bade farewell to the Navy team, urging each other to keep practicing if they wanted to improve, and we went back to our mundane day jobs.

The Sea king helicopter is lifted clear of the water and secured to the bow of the recovery vessel 'Kinbrace'

The Recovery Operation as seen from the top of Chesil Bank. The diving team is situated in Gemini boat.

Kenya, Part 1: Military Diving Reconnaissance

Around this time, I was summoned to the Commanding Officer's office. He said he was keen to get the diving team away to do a useful project and did I have any ideas. So I rattled off some locations, but only in Europe.

At that time we had a sub unit in Kenya on a civil engineering project, so I casually mentioned Kenya at the end of the list of possibilities. 'Now there's an idea', he said. He was flying out there to visit the unit in two days time. He told me to get packed and join him on a reconnaissance to look for suitable tasks.

I ended up in Mombasa and on the Diani coast, looked at several potential tasks and got a good overview of the area. As you will read later, we eventually did a project, but not in Mombasa. However, my experience with Mombasa was to be very beneficial to me later.

Belize, Part 1: Operational Military Tour of Duty

1974 was proving to be a busy year for me. First in Scotland, then Kenya, and now to Belize. My troop was being sent to Belize for a six month tour. The warm climate and location is always a big draw for the lads, and I particularly looked forward to the diving opportunities. I had never dived the Caribbean.

Our home for the duration was to be in a camp alongside the international airport in Belize, brilliantly named Airport Camp, and situated a few miles outside Belize City. Once settled, we started to look into the adventure training possibilities. The coastline of Belize's mainland is not one of sandy beaches. It is mostly mangrove swamp, and the areas immediately north and south of Belize City are badly polluted by the Belize River, which enters the sea there. The river is the main means of rubbish and sewage disposal for the city. There are, however, hundreds of small sandy islands of various sizes called cays. These were the Bounty advert paradise islands of dreams. Belize also possesses the second largest barrier reef in the world. The diving potential was unlimited. The Army's presence in Belize was due, I believe, to the old days when it was called British Honduras. We had a garrison as protection and to assist in hurricane relief. This meant we had boats, outboard motors and all the equipment to go with them. There was plenty of scope for adventure training, but particularly water related training.

It was very common for the smaller units, sections or troops to arrange a day on the cays for themselves as a break from routine. They would sunbathe, snorkel and have a barbecue. It was a fantastic way to unwind. There was a good system of access to boats and commuting to the cays. Once clear of the river effluent, the water became turquoise and crystal clear. The garrison had a central pool of sub aqua equipment which, at that time, was little used.

At the first opportunity I sought out the sub aqua kit, checked it over and made a note of what wanted doing. It was not too bad. As most divers know, all dive plans can be ruined by not having a simple piece of kit, which only costs pennies, but without which you cannot dive. I had long since included a plastic box of such items in all my travels. The favourites were o-rings, but I also included mask straps, fin straps and various threaded blanks, maintenance oils, lubes, silicon, spanners, scissors and repair kits. The list is endless, and I knew that I could use this spares box to keep the show on the road. There have been times when I would have given my eye teeth for something small and insignificant, such as a small rubber o-ring.

Some of the world's best diving is totally isolated, away from civilisation, electricity or drinking water. Therefore, if you need something you have not brought with you, you do without. One of the most inventive pieces of improvisation or making do I came across was when we had completely run out of o-rings. Sometimes you can get away with turning them over. We even rotated the good ones until we had no more. We looked everywhere, and tried many ideas just to keep on the road. The only thing we found, which worked and proved safe, was an old piece of rubber garden hose the same diameter as the o-rings. By cutting this into slices of the correct size we found it worked well. The only risk with improvisation is when things go seriously wrong. Even if it has nothing to do with the improvisation, some follow up enquiries can deem this unnecessary risk taking or unsanctioned repairs. I think the answer is to use them yourself and test them to your own satisfaction in a safe environment. In the case of the hose o-rings, they could be left under pressure with a regulator connected for hours if necessary and the cylinder contents regularly checked without having to dive with them. If they held a charge and there were no blowouts (sudden rapid loss of air), they could be tested in the water on a diver. If you are the supervisor or instructor you should do the testing.

    As well as the cays and coral reef, Belize boasts a phenomenon that is found nowhere else in the world. The Blue Hole is positioned centrally in Lighthouse Reef, approximately sixty miles due east of Belize City. Lighthouse Reef and the Blue

Hole are best viewed from the air. Imagine Lighthouse Reef as a soft oval shape of shallow turquoise water, perhaps six kilometres long and one to two kilometres wide, surrounded by dark, deep water. In the centre of the reef is an ink black circle, perhaps two hundred and forty metres in diameter, with its rim almost completely covered by shallow coral. There are two breaks in the coral heads around the rim that are big enough to allow small craft access to the deep water of the Blue Hole (and not so small craft). The good ship Calypso was motored in there by Jacques Cousteau for the filming of a documentary (Calypso is a converted United States Navy minesweeper). It is an awesome sight. It is, in fact, a former cave whose roof collapsed at the end of an ice age due to the rise in sea levels. It is four hundred and seven feet deep. The origins and age of the cave were proved during a Cousteau expedition in 1972. They recovered a broken stalactite from the cave floor using a submersible robot. By analysing the stalactite, they were able to accurately date the cave. The fact that stalactites are there at all proved that it once was a cave. Nowadays the Blue Hole is a world famous diving attraction, and Belize is a very popular eco-holiday destination, within easy reach of the United States and Mexico. However, this part of the book relates to 1974, and there were no dive boats, groups or clubs as far as I am aware. I never met any other divers there, apart from the ones I was training, so it really was like breaking new ground.

The Army's work out there was not excessive, and there were plenty of opportunities to pursue adventure training.

Airport Camp also had a swimming pool, which was handy for practising basic drills. The diving kit, held centrally, was under used in those days, but the masks, snorkels, fins and bootees had been well used for snorkelling, and were in a dire state. Back then there were no dive shops in Belize, but some shops did sell snorkelling gear of varying standards, so it was possible to replace these items when needed. The biggest single problem there was lads using the snorkelling kit after applying insect repellent. The insect repellent damages and eventually destroys rubber, and the soft rubber on the mask seals was particularly vulnerable.

I assembled a group of divers and touted for a dive boat. It did not need to be a live aboard. We would only use it to commute to the dive sites. We planned to go to Lighthouse Reef and stay in government owned timber houses on Half Moon Cay, a beautiful tropical island situated at the southernmost tip of Lighthouse Reef. The cay housed an old, wrought iron, Victorian lighthouse (it now has a new one) and an old, eccentric, Belizian lighthouse keeper called Melvin A Coleman. Around the base of the lighthouse were three windblown and sun bleached timber houses. They made ideal accommodation and administrative base for us, and I used them on several future occasions. Melvin was a great character and a very generous and likeable human being. He was the only inhabitant of the island, so whenever we arrived he had saved up all his talking for us. He spoke English with a Creole Caribbean accent, and nothing was too much trouble for him. He usually lived there with no company except a radio. That radio was probably the only difference between him and Alexander Selkirk (the original Robinson Crusoe)! I remember him to this day with great affection. The cay was an excellent base. One of the shores was always in the lee of the wind and swell, so it could always be dived. It was located at the southern tip of Lighthouse Reef, which meant we were also alongside deep-water drop-off s topped with sandy shallows and coral heads. A few miles to the north lay the Blue Hole. In a sentence, it was one of the most perfect dive sites in the world. It had everything. Another great attribute of the Blue Hole was that it was perfect for carrying out deep diving techniques and training. You had vertical descent and ascent, no current, no hazard from other shipping and visibility was crystal clear.

Spare rooms in the houses made ideal classrooms, and all the houses had kitchens. You just had to bring your own gas. We ate a mixture of tinned composite rations and fresh local produce, usually bought from the Mennonite farmers. There were two portable Poseidon compressors and the army diving kit had a Dunlop compressor. We also had Avon drysuits with us, which you may think strange or unnecessary, particularly in that heat and warm water. However, there was a chance of us being tasked in polluted water (or even in the Belize River), and you would not want to be in a neoprene suit in those conditions. We had full-face masks for the same reason.

We augmented our rations with fresh fish. The boat we hired came with a very experienced operator called Demitrio Mehia, or Demi for short. He took a load off my shoulders in responsibility for the boat handling, access and anchor points. He was also excellent at snorkelling and a competent sports diver. The boat was called Carib Gipsy. Demi owned a spear gun.

The last dive or snorkel of each day would be Demi, going in to hopefully snare something for the pot. Often, we had a sundown barbecue of Nassau grouper or jewfish. It really does not get much better than that. We would always, of course, include Melvin in the festivities; he was always part of the team.

In those days spear fishing was a regular pursuit for many of divers. I never ever got in to it. This was mainly because I was nearly always supervising novices and, believe me, the last thing you wanted in such a situation was some idiot diving with a spear gun, even if that idiot was me. There was also the problem that spear fishing attracted large predatory fish, which usually arrived in an agitated state expecting an easy meal. This was another situation to be avoided, especially when with a group of novices. So, in the main, I did not allow spear fishing whilst I had divers in the water. I read all the accounts, particularly from Australia, o f spear fishermen attacked by sharks. They would carry their haul of half-dead fish around with them and then wonder why they were attacked (look at the clues here folks).

By way of confession, during my time as instructor at the diving school at Kiel, my then boss John Briffitt was a spear fisherman, and he urged me to have a go. The Baltic is a relatively dead sea for inshore sea life, and all I managed to bag was a Blenny: not only no use to eat, but too small. I felt horrible looking at it squirm on the trident and sorry for it, and as painlessly as possible released it, whereupon it swam away. I tell you this story reluctantly, as I do not want to compromise my hardened killer image, so do not tell anyone else. Right?

The expeditions to Lighthouse Reef were usually a week to ten days long. During the six-month tour I organised three separate expeditions. One of them was for the army air corps lads who controlled the helicopters. Now, to have use of a helicopter was awesome, and on three occasions I flew out to Lighthouse Reef and back over the Turneffe Islands and the Blue Hole. The helicopters the Army used then Sioux helicopters, which had a big glass fishbowl type cockpit, giving you great visibility and photographic opportunities.

I got to know the various dive sites very well, swam amongst the stalactites in the Blue Hole, and amongst manta rays, barracuda and sharks. I dived on vertical drop-off s into the dark blue yonder and saw all there was to see. Jacques Cousteau was the first ever to organise an expedition to the Blue Hole in 1972. The next three expeditions were organised by me with lads from the army in 1974 and 1975, a snippet of factual information of which I am quite proud.

Half Moon Cay on the southern edge of Lighthouse reef. The timber built government houses can be seen, which provided us with accommodation during the expeditions. Note the wreck aground on the eastern edge of the reef.

The old Victorian lighthouse with an Army Sioux Helicopter hovering above it.

Nowadays, the Blue Hole is a world famous dive site. There is plenty of research information known about it. In those days there was nothing. You pioneered your own experience and knowledge.

At that time I was not an underwater photographer. Come to think of it, even though I own and sometimes dive with a camera, I am still not much of an underwater photographer, but I try my best.

Situated due south from Belize City are two large lagoons, spookily called Northern and Southern Lagoon. They lie parallel to the Caribbean. The two lagoons are separated by a strip of land, on which runs a forest track. The track runs between the lagoons directly to the sea. At the place where it reaches the sea is a timber piled jetty. Alongside that jetty were the remnants of an old jetty, with its rickety timber piles sticking out like a row of rotten teeth. The old jetty was an obstruction, which meant that any boats coming alongside the newer jetty could only do so along one side. The main use for the jetty was to load up the produce, bananas I think, from a huge plantation behind the lagoons. As they did not have any cranes, all the loading was done by hand. The normal practise was for the boat to come alongside and load that side up to amidships. Then the boat would move to the end of the jetty, turn around and come back alongside, thus enabling the workers to load the empty side.

Our job was, quite simply, to remove the old piles. I needed to do a reconnaissance to assess the job, a plan, stores list and time schedule. I booked a helicopter and set off with snorkelling equipment. This meant that if I needed to have a closer look I could snorkel down, as it was only in the shallows next to the beach.

The Army classed such tasks as Military Aid to the Civil Community (MACC), and they were often good training opportunities for us. It was of mutual benefit. There would be no payment involved, but sometimes a nice meal, crate of beer or, I imagine in this case, all the bananas you could eat. MACC tasks are not as common in the United Kingdom or Europe, as you start to step on the toes of the local work force. In places like Belize, we were much less constrained.

Whilst flying down the coast, the pilot and I witnessed an amazing sight. A very large hammerhead shark was swimming right in to the beach, less than four feet from the waters edge. Between it and the beach was a large stingray with one of its wings completely out of the water. The shark was frantically trying to catch the ray, but could not get close enough because the water was only a few inches deep. It was thrashing around, causing lots of spray. Most of its squirming body was out of the water. It was an awesome spectacle. The pilot dropped the helicopter out of the sky like a stone, and we hovered above the two of them. The skids of the aircraft were within a foot of the shark. I could have leaned out of the doorway (there was no door) and touched the shark. The turbulence caused by the rotor blades added to the frenzy. Eventually we elevated and flew off . We must have been there for up to three minutes. As we flew off I was speechless (that takes some doing!), and looked down and noticed my camera was on my lap. I had forgotten it, so there are no photographs. Maybe I am not as clever as I think I am. The shark was almost the length of the aircraft, certainly four and a half metres, perhaps five. I have never witnessed anything like that again, ever.

I returned with the required information. The job was well within our capabilities. I then received news that my father had died. He had been hospitalised after a fall from a stepladder and never recovered. It was a terrible loss for me. All institutions have their simplistic rules. As I was married, my father was no longer considered my next of kin, so I ended up having to finance the trip home to attend his funeral myself. I did receive some help, with the use of military flights on what was called the indulgence system, but still had to pay. Such things stick in the craw.

When I arrived back in Belize the jetty task had been done. I had a good understudy and had given all the information to him. He did the task satisfactorily, and when I next saw him he was distinctly off colour from eating free bananas.

In between dives I was still a section commander and we took part in an inter-section competition in the jungle. These things can be very good fun, whilst bonding the section together. Belize had some fantastic natural features: caves, rapids, jungle, cliff s, swamps and mountains, as well as the beauty of the cays. During the competition we lived in what we carried and were tasked differently each day. We built a footbridge for a local village, producing the raw materials ourselves from the jungle. Whilst doing this, some sap from a tree we had cut stuck to my wrist and killed the skin beneath. There was a patch of black dead skin, which remained unsightly for over a week. When the competition was finished I visited the doctor at Airport Camp who told me that the sap had been very poisonous. Had it touched my eyes, it would have blinded me for life. The medicine he gave me cleared it up, but to this day I still have a scar. It was whilst on this competition, lying in my basha (a self-made shelter) with my ear stuck to a little world service radio, that I heard the news that Muhammad Ali had regained his title by defeating George Foreman in Zaire.

Experiences like the tree sap, and many other lessons I learned, would hold me in good stead when, years later, I was to run my own survival school.

Another task in Belize was recovering the body of a young soldier who was in the signals. He had been with his troop on a day's cay trip. Alcohol had been consumed, and he got into difficulties whilst snorkelling and drowned. We travelled out there. The mood is always sombre on such occasions and recalling where to start looking is always a problem. Every witness has his own interpretation of what happened and judging distances across water it is not easy. I received a good sighting and down I went. Within fifteen minutes I found him, lying on the sand like a doll.

It was not too difficult. The visibility, even though it was overcast, was fifteen metres. I secured my buoy line rope around his ankles and signalled five bells. The people topside knew that I had found him and the boat stood nearby. I surfaced, signalled, got into the boat and helped pull him up. He was already stiff. He was buried in Belize.

Whilst on Half Moon Cay we had a visit from the Commanding Officer (CO), the one of the bag of scallops fame. He did not have enough time to dive as he was flying out the next day, but he had a fabulous snorkel among the coral heads and found some dried fan coral from beach combing for his wife's flower arranging. He left us a happy man, and again expressed that he was pleased that opportunities were being fully taken.

Towards the end of the tour I went on an errand to Belize City. I was sitting in the back of a land rover trying not to fall through the big hole where the floor was supposed to be. I looked up and saw that a car was following us that had just come from the airport. I looked at the passenger and thought 'I know this face'. Quite unbelievably, it was Jacques Cousteau! I smiled and waved, and he smiled and waved back. When we got to the waterfront I could see the white-hulled outline of Calypso, which was anchored off Belize City. I was stunned. The next day I was standing on a small motor boat en route to spend some time on Calypso. Cousteau was out there to study the differences in the coral reef between night and day, and asked any divers with local knowledge to come and visit. I did not need to be asked twice, so I was on a boat en route to Calypso.

This next passage is quite embarrassing. Also on the boat was a small guy wearing a cowboy hat and a leather jacket with strips hanging down along the arms, a bit like Tonto in the Lone Ranger (remember him?). Behind him was another guy who looked as if he was just commuting to his job at the bank. Striking up friendly conversation, I asked what he did for a living. He said 'I'm his agent'. I said 'Blimey, I didn't realise Jacques Cousteau had an agent'. When we arrived on Calypso I went up to the bridge and started talking over the chart table with Jacques

Cousteau and Falco, his chief diver. Meanwhile, the guy in the cowboy hat was dishing out eight-track tapes (remember them?) to the crew. There was also a load of re-supply kit on the motor boat, which we helped to offload.

I spent about eight hours on board and had my photograph taken with Jacques Cousteau, Falco et al. It was a fabulous time. I was given a tour of the ship, including the little glass bubble underwater at the bow. They needed it, with an observer inside, to guide them through the shallows into the Blue Hole. The photograph of Jacques Cousteau and me now adorns one of my logbooks (I wonder if the same photograph is in one of his logbooks and he tells everyone 'Look, here is me with Tony Liddicoat'?). Two days later I learned that the guy in the cowboy hat was called John Denver. At the time I had never heard of him, but he had just released a record called 'Calypso' and was visiting the boat with his agent to promote it. I have to say, he was quite unassuming and a genuinely nice guy. If I had known then how famous he was, I would have asked for his autograph. As it was, I only got Jacques Cousteau's and Falco's. Oh well!

An aerial photograph of the Blue Hole is on the back cover of the book.

Standing and talking with Jacques Cousteau on Calypso.

The six months seemed to fly by (apart from losing my father).

It was now 1974 and I was twenty-six years old already. Little did I know, I had not seen the last of Belize.

When we returned home we had some well-earned leave with our families. Annie could not drive and it was a nonsense having the car parked outside doing nothing, while she had to bus everywhere. The priority was to get her driving and pass the test. This she did.

Scotland, Part 2: The Blasting of a Deep Water Channel

It was 1974 and I was still at Maidstone and running the diving team (as well being a section commander). The Commanding Officer still had ambitions of getting the diving team away. In April I set off on a reconnaissance with two of my team and an officer to the Outer Hebrides. We went in a Land Rover pulling a trailer full of diving kit to enable us to carry out underwater surveys.

The officer was a non-diver and I think he was with us because he could do joined up writing. My only previous experience in Scotland was the aforementioned adventure training in Plockton. We drove northwards, and through some absolutely stunning scenery, to Oban.

The main ferry service for travelling around the islands is provided by ferries of the Caledonian Macbrayne company (it does not get any more Scottish than that!). We had pre-booked, and at Oban early one morning we were waiting on a slipway to load onto the ferry. A transit van from a local bakery pulled up, and an employee took out three trays of cakes to take on board. They probably carried them to save paying for the vehicle on the ferry. No sooner had the transit left, than the wind picked up the trays and tipped them upside down. The cakes were scattered everywhere. The employee meticulously collected them all from the floor, put them back into the tray and sat on them to prevent a recurrence, then loaded the trays and himself on to the ferry and delivered them to Castlebay on the island of Barra. So here is a tip for all Castlebay residents. Do not eat mainland doughnuts, and do not say you have not been warned.

Our aim was to travel northwards through the Outer Hebrides chain, and see if there were any prospective jobs along the MACC system. The Army had undertaken a task previously on the island of Benbecula, which had a guided missile range on it. Army divers had been employed to recover rocket drones, which had landed and sunk out at sea. The Army has a live firing rocket range on the islands, so was no stranger there.

Castlebay is a picture postcard town, a small scallop-shaped bay with a small island in the bay. On the island is an ancient castle. The castle is the main seat of one of the clans, but my memory fails and I forget which one (it begins with a Mac something!). The local gossip was all about the fact that the island and castle had recently been purchased by an American, a move which went down like a lead fart with the locals.

The town and bay are overlooked by a large hill, which acts as a backdrop. Halfway up this hill is a statue of the Virgin Mary holding the baby Jesus. I was told it was called 'Our Lady of the Isles', and was there to bring safety and luck to the local fishermen.

The view from the statue is breathtaking. I have described previously how the scenery and water clarity in Scotland is fabulous. If anything, the water clarity here in the Outer Hebrides was even better.

There are a few small islands to the south of Barra. The main one is called Vatersay. The day after arriving, we were taken across to Vatersay to look at the possibility of building a jetty capable of taking a car ferry. The strip of water between the two islands was very interesting. In this waterway in 1941 the SS Politician, en route to America, ran aground and eventually sank. On board were two hundred and sixty four thousand bottles of whiskey. The wreck became part of local folklore and was made famous in the film Whiskey Galore. Whilst crossing the water, it was pointed out to me where the wreck now lies. The current and tidal rip at the time, through the Sound of Vatersay, was quite ferocious.

As if that is not enough of historic wreck stories, just on the lip of Castle Bay is the wreck of an old steam puffer. With its inebriated captain at the helm, it steamed away from the jetty in Castle Bay at full speed astern in a straight line on to the rocks on the other side, was holed and sank. It has got to be difficult insuring a ship around those parts. The beaches are amongst the best in the world. There is a big flat beach at the north of Barra, which is used as the local airport.

After the delights of Barra we caught a ferry north to Lochboisdale, and drove through South Uist, Benbecula and North Uist, to the port of Lochmaddy. We then caught the ferry to the Isle of Harris and Lewis, and arrived at Tarbert. At Tarbert we were asked to reconnoitre the fishing harbour on the island of Scalpay.

At that time there was only a small car ferry connecting the island with the main island (today there is a bridge).

The tiny fishing village had a problem. As fishing boats over the years had got bigger, their draught had become deeper, and a couple of them had hit rocks when entering the harbour. They wanted the obstructions removed and the harbour channel deepened. It had good potential as an MACC task. I dived to ascertain what could be done, but the whole area was covered in a forest of kelp, so little could be seen.

I did notice paths cut through the top of the kelp, which looked as if they had been cut with a large pair of scissors. They had in fact been cut by the propellers of the fishing boats. The area had a huge tidal rise and fall, some seventeen feet during the spring tides. Whilst there was no problem with harbour access at high water, what they wanted was safe and unrestricted access at all times.

Whilst on Scalpay we were hosted by the head of the island's council, and had tea in his cottage. They were lovely people, and made us feel very welcome. We were all crammed into their small kitchen and chatting away, when his wife appeared with a freshly baked fruitcake. It smelt delicious. As the cake appeared, Ady, one of the team's divers, relaxed back in his chair and crashed his head upwards into a wall cupboard that he had obviously forgotten was there. It was such a whack that the hosts reached for the first aid kit asking if he was alright. 'Sure', he replied, 'I'm fine. It was just the excitement of the fruitcake'. He never used to get out much, that lad.

We looked at another potential task at Port of Ness, which is the most northerly point of the Isle of Lewis. A concrete jetty had been badly damaged and holed, making it unsafe for heavier loads. They wanted the damage made good and the holes refilled with concrete. Whilst we were there on the reconnaissance, we saw the waves coming in to the cliff base on the headland, and the white spume spray of the waves shooting upwards over the cliff tops. This area certainly knew bad weather. We had spent a very enjoyable fourteen days on the reconnaissance, and departed Stornaway by ferry to Ullapool and drove back to Kent. Two months later we were to start on deepening the fishing harbour on Scalpay.

Back in Maidstone we prepared the stores needed. I was still employed in my other job of section commander, which was very demanding at times. It involved dealing with people, my people, and of course human problems are not like paperwork that can be put in a tray and dealt with when convenient. They need to be given priority, and if you are to expect the best from people, they are entitled to expect the best from you. Whilst this is totally correct, it is very time consuming.

I already knew that Scalpay was isolated. Even the main island would not be able to supply the wide and varied list of spares we may need.

Scalpay did not even have a shop so, apart from killer fruitcake, anything else we might need was a boat ride and car drive away. We took three assault boats and motors, two high-pressure compressors, all the diving equipment, buoys, anchors, cordage, etc. We used the old school hall as accommodation, bringing our own camp beds and sleeping systems. The hall had a cooker and small kitchen, ablutions and large shower. A shower is important after spending all day in a dry suit (they were still neck entry).

The fishing harbour of Scalpay, we were accommodated in the school house at the end of the jetty.

Inside the school room where we lived, slept and ate in one room.

I asked for a mechanic and cook to be included in the team so that the diving team could concentrate on the diving. The young cook came up to me after a briefing and said that he would be delighted if he could have a go at diving. I told him it was not a problem, but that his enjoyment and the under water conditions of his dive would be directly related to the standard of the food we were eating! I also let it slip that, on my last task, the cook had mysteriously drowned and they had still not found the body. The food was excellent, supplemented by fresh scallops, and he proved to be a very good novice diver who subsequently took up sport diving. We also took an army mechanic. As I said earlier, if the outboard motors or compressors did not work, then nothing would get done. We gave priority to keeping them working. Maintenance, repair and servicing during the project had to be kept under control. Luckily, the weather was generally fine.

The tidal rise and fall was quite severe, and one morning mid project we awoke after a rare storm to find two of the assault boats with outboard motors had turned turtle. The securing line from the bow was too long, and the boats had been blown to one side and caught on some rocks. When the tide ebbed, they ended up rocking to and fro on the rocks in the storm swell and slipped stern first under water as the rising tide came in.

The boats and engines had been under water for hours. I feared the worst. I discussed it with the mechanic, Nick Burgess. We had propellers, shear pins and the usual list of spares, but immersion for hours in salt water could have caused a whole different set of problems. The electrics would probably be beyond repair. Groan. Nick said 'Get the lads to recover the engines and bring them up here, and I will do what I can'. We were down to one working boat and my mind was racing through various ideas to replace, beg, borrow or steal a back up outboard motor (or two).

In the meantime we set to work in the main channel. After a couple of hours I looked up to see, in the distance, a boat speeding towards us. When it got closer I could see it was one of our assault boats, being driven at full tilt by Nick. He took a wide berth of the dive site and sped the boat to and fro. It was fantastic to see, and I knew we were back on the road. It would have been a bit picky of me to bollock him for not wearing a life jacket. He sped back to the jetty and by the end of the day both outboard motors had been repaired and were back to full use. Outstanding! Well done Nick.

*Loading the assault boat for the days dive
(Note the very long mooring ropes to contend with the 17' tidal range)*

Pre dive checks before entering the water.

Preparation activity in the boat

Detonation of the some of the main charges

If anyone reading this ever finds themselves in such a situation, then do not be told by anyone that all is lost. Nick had first submerged the engines in fresh water, then removed all the electrics and dried them in a warm oven. He carefully cleaned all the contacts, and then painstakingly replaced and rebuilt them .All was not lost. You just need know-how and the will to do it.

At the start of the task we made up a jackstay (long length of cordage) and weighted it at intervals from the boat along the proposed centreline of the channel. When pulled tight, with an anchor at each end, it provided the divers with a reference point and direction. We checked to see that the jackstay was on the bottom for its whole length and not snagged anywhere. The next problem was the removal of the kelp forest along the jackstay to a width of eight metres. To do this, I placed two divers alongside each other, one holding the jackstay in their left hand the other holding it in their right. Thus, when spread out, the span of both divers combined would be some four metres. I gave them each a machete to work along the jackstay cutting through the kelp. It was important to keep both divers progressing together. I did not want the scenario of two divers in a thick kelp forest wielding machetes and moving towards each other, so emphasis was placed on co-ordination even if it meant working a little slower.

During this task one of the divers came upon a huge lobster. It was an all of a sudden moment. The lobster approached his head, pincers at the ready. He was quite startled, and his immediate reaction was to whack it with the machete. Of course, the lobster took exception to this so it was fight on. Jock the diver won, and he brought the lobster to the surface and put it in the boat. It weighed about eight pounds, which I know is not a record, but it was big enough for us. Jock actually sold it to a hotel in Tarbert.

Locals told us that the biggest Scottish lobster on record was caught in the little fishing bay of Scalpay where we were working. It used to be a port of call for the Caledonian Macbrayne ferries, and the remains of the old timber piled jetty were still there. It was whilst the ferry was alongside the jetty that a small boy was fishing with a piece of string that had a piece of bacon rind at the end. The record lobster crimped the bacon in its pincer, and was pulled up out of the water. As soon as the dive team heard this they approached me and asked if they could have danger money due to the fact that monsters of the deep frequented the work site. I told them to eff off.

Eventually the kelp was cleared to a width of eight metres. We could then see the problem. There was a slight contour rise, and several large granite boulders on the top of the rise. We decided to break down and fragment the boulders using explosives. After a detailed reconnaissance we knew the size of the problem. We could then estimate how many explosive charges were needed, and where they should be placed.

Having made the plan, we arranged with a local quarry to use their explosive bunker as a store for our own military explosives and detonators. Such items are subject to special storage regulations and have to be kept separate. It is not just a case of putting them in a cardboard box in the kitchen! We altered our routine to include taking a boat to the main island, collecting the explosives and detonators, and bringing them back to be prepared for firing. We also marked the explosive placement sites with anchors and buoy lines for ease of finding and placing. I wanted to detonate the charges when the tide was in, thus giving a maximum tamping effect of the water and reducing the blast effect on the local community. We also told the local community when to expect the explosions, so there would not be large unexpected explosions whilst people were lighting their gas cookers!

We initiated the explosives from the surface using a timber raft attached to the pre-positioned anchor line. This made it easier to check misfires and enabled controlled initiation when everyone was clear (apart from the boat carrying the initiation party). It was a system that worked well. We had one misfire though, which the initiation set had detonated, but not the main charge. I waited the contact safety time and dived down to check it out. The detonation cord, which detonates instantaneously, had cut itself. It needs to be in a fairly straight line. If it is kinked around a sharp corner the detonation is so instant that it tends to cut itself at the kink. We quickly attached a new initiation set and blew the charges.

Another incident was right out of Monty Python. I initiated the explosive charge, which meant igniting a slow burning fuse. The fuse time is calculated to allow plenty of time for the initiation crew to get well away to safety before the main charges blow. Usually it is a piece of cake; outboard motor ticking over, initiation set lit, engine in reverse, away from the smoking fuse then into forward gear and zoom to safety. All went according to this sequence, apart from the zoom to safety. When we did the zoom to safety bit the engine stalled and cut out. We were left floating aimlessly above seventy kilograms of explosives, which were about to detonate, with no means of propulsion. I instantly told the crew to grab paddles and get us to the nearest shoreline, pointing in the direction I wanted to go. I have to say that there were very few instances in my army life when I received, or expected, instant obedience to an order. This time, however, the lads exceeded themselves. The paddles resembled bees' wings. I think I could have water-skied behind if I had wanted. Meanwhile, we worked feverishly on the engine for all we were worth. We reached the shoreline and up went the explosive charges. Everything was fine. We tilted the engine inboard to work on it and discovered the lifeline rope from the standby diver was wrapped around the propeller, which had caused it to stall and cut out. That was a relief because it gave us someone to blame, and Rick the standby diver was fined a round of drinks. During the frenetic paddling and activity on the boat, one of the team burst forth with the theme fromthe television series Hawaii Five-O, 'Dah dah dah dah Daaah Daaah...'.I remember thinking at the time 'There's another candidate for a round of drinks', but nobody owned up to it. We prepared the charges daily, placed them and detonated them, so they were not usually in the water long enough to be affected by the sea. The plastic explosive we used was PE4, a military explosive that was water resistant and malleable. As a precaution we waterproofed the explosives by inserting them into condoms.

Once fragmented, the boulders were no longer an obstacle in the channel. By simply blasting the large boulders, we increased the working depth of the channel by more than one metre as requested. Our last task was to mark the channel using leading lights. These were two triangular road signs, white with a red border, on metal posts. One of the triangles was inverted.

I placed a surface swimmer in the middle of each end of the newly blown channel alongside a buoy that was attached to an anchor. Upon a given hand signal they pulled the buoy lines until they were vertical. I then fixed my attention on the triangle post on land, which was held by one of the team. I gave directional arm signals until I could see that the two swimmers in the water at each end of the channel, and the man on the shore, were in a straight line. When this was done, we had the position for one of the channel indicators on land. We then duplicated this procedure using another team member with the other pole and the inverted triangle. This one was positioned higher up the hill. When all four markers were in line, we knew that the channel was accurately marked.

If the channel was used at night sailors only had to put lights on the triangles. Anyone wishing to enter the harbour by using the safe channel had to line up the land markers so they were vertical to each other. This system is called leading lights.

During the last week the Commanding Officer visited us. It was he of the bag of scallops fame. He flew up in an army Cessna light aircraft. We gave his group as good a lunch as we could, including a scallop au gratin starter. The CO had been enormously supportive to me, and the diving team, during his tenure. His name was John Awford, and if he ever reads this book I would like him to know that his support was very much appreciated.

The Cessna pilot was a character. He said that he was tasked mainly with VIP flights and, of course, there were no toilet facilities on board. If passengers were caught short during a long flight, to one side a funnel was attached to a corrugated hose, which they could urinate into, and it was pumped out of the plane. He explained that two days earlier he had flown a general and his wife. During the flight the wife had wanted to talk to him, so she picked up the funnel and started talking into it. I imagine you could have sold tickets for that!

On the final evening the whole team was invited out for a night on the local community. Appropriately enough, we all piled onto one of their fishing trawlers and sailed across the water to Tarbert and the local inn. It was a nice evening and most of the community attended. We returned to Scalpay harbour in the trawler at dark o'clock. The main thing was that the tide had gone out, and getting out of the boat meant a vertical climb up a metal-runged ladder attached to the jetty. We started to ascend one by one. Nick Burgess, the now famous but inebriated mechanic, joined the ladder queue. It was a climb of about fifteen rungs. There were two or three people on the ladder at any one time. When Nick was climbing the ladder the person at the top became stuck. The next person down stopped, and the next, but Nick carried on climbing, slowly and methodically. The person above him was the wife of one of the councillors. Nick continued his upward progress, and we all watched in silence, looking at the ladder and wondering what was causing the hold-up. We watched, in slow time, as Nick's head and shoulders disappeared underneath her calf length skirt. He stopped when he could go no further. The hold-up cleared itself as did Nick, eventually. He said afterwards that he was trying to figure out why it had suddenly gone dark. Well done Nick.

Job done. We bade farewell to Scalpay and the Outer Hebrides. I brought back a crate of beautiful tasty kippers, purchased on the quayside at Stornaway. Who says romance is dead.

Annie was pregnant again, and on the twenty sixth of January 1976 we had a daughter, Sarah, who proved to be the world's cheekiest kid, and still is despite a university degree and a posh job in the city!

In 1977 the Army eventually came to its senses and promoted me to sergeant. I had spent more than seven years as a corporal (the average is three to four), and the promotion came with a burbled letter trying to explain how I had served my punishment for leaving the Army to go into commercial diving. Yeah right!

Berlin

With the promotion came a move. I was posted to Berlin.

Berlin at that time was a walled city. It was a little island of democracy and capitalism amidst the austere world of eastern European communism. Within this walled island was not only a beautiful and vibrant city, but also a token military presence for each of the allies; the United Kingdom, the United States and France. When I say token, I mean just that. On the other side of the wall we were outnumbered in everything by a trillion to one. All that the Russians would need to do, in the event of hostilities, would be to place Prisoner of War Camp signs on the wall. However, we practised playing at war, and I also ran the army diving team there.

Within a few weeks of arriving I saw a Defence Council Instruction (DCI), which is like a military chain letter, requesting divers to attend a diving expedition to Mombasa. I asked my Officer Commanding (OC) if he would he give me permission to throw my hat in the ring and apply. I mentioned that there was no guarantee I would be selected. He had only known me a few months, but said 'Listen Sergeant Liddicoat. We both know that if you apply, then you'll certainly be selected'. It was a nice compliment, but I did not share his optimism. I filled in the application form and emphasised my previous Mombasa experience and what I hoped to bring to the table. The list was quite thorough. I knew it was a subaqua sport diving expedition. I also knew that there were not likely to be many others with commercial and military diving qualifications. As they planned an archaeological excavation of an old wreck using surface demand diving equipment, I hoped my extensive experience with that system would help my application. I could also offer my compressor skills, boat handling, dive supervising and practical diving skills. I was hopeful, but nothing else.

Kenya, Part 2: The Mombasa Wreck Excavation, 1977

Within two weeks I heard that I had been selected. The dates for the expedition were the sixth of January until the tenth of April 1977. The expedition comprised twelve men good and true, four each from the Army, Navy and Air Force. We assembled at RAF Brize Norton in Oxfordshire. It was the first time we had all been together as a team. During this time every year, the Army undertakes various training exercises in Kenya. There are always military aircraft flying out and back, so we hitched a ride out and managed to get a lot of the expedition freight out as well.

We were interviewed by Kenyan Radio and started to get to know each other. It was an exciting time.

The next morning we took off in a CI5O Hercules transport plane. We had an overnight stop in Athens. It was there that I got to know the expedition leader, Alec Tilley. Alec was a

Lieutenant Commander in the Navy and a real English gentleman. He had, at some time in his youth, fallen in love in Athens, and we had a stroll around the back streets retracing his old haunts. A warm balmy Mediterranean evening with a carafe of house wine in a cobbled back street overlooked by the Acropolis is a clear memory I have to this day. Alec was great company and a true romantic. The next morning we took off again, stopping at Khartoum to refuel. Hours later we landed in Nairobi.

We were given Landrover vehicles on to which we loaded our equipment and ourselves, and set off. The three hundred and twenty mile journey from Nairobi to Mombasa took us from the dry heat of Nairobi, to the tropical humidity of the coast, through the stunning game park of Tsavo. The road runs parallel to the famous railway, which, during construction, lost eleven workers to man-eating lions. This story is told in the book The Man-Eaters of Tsavo[2] by J M Paterson. The train is now called the Man-Eater Express. Nairobi is some two thousand metres above sea level, so the road drops down in gentle stages. The vegetation is the main indication of its proximity to the sea. Mombasa is the only natural deep-water harbour in East Africa, and is an island. To the south Diani Beach, which connects to Mombasa with a ferry at Likoni. To the north Nyali beach, which was, in

---

[2] J M Paterson, *The Man-Eaters of Tsavo*, (England, Saint Martin's Press)

those days, connected to Mombasa by a large pontoon bridge with a timber 1986 roadway. The width of the roadway was just wide enough to allow two cars to pass.

Our accommodation was a disused agricultural showground on the north coast next to the shoreline. We commuted across the water to the wreck site. The excavation site was just off shore in front of Fort Jesus, a huge citadel built by the Portuguese to protect their interests in Mombasa and their trade routes to the Dutch East Indies. The area is steeped in history. It was whilst coming to relieve a besieged Fort Jesus in 1697 that the San Antonio de Tanna ran aground and eventually sank in front of the fort (records are hazy from this period). A couple of centuries later, at the request of the Kenyan Government working with the National Museum of Kenya and the Institute of Nautical Archaeology (INA), a magnetometer survey was done. The result showed a large concentration of ferrous metal in one place. It was thought that this could be cannon balls concreted together. Fort Jesus is now a museum where artefacts are displayed. The wreck site was on a steep slope. Mombasa is a very deep harbour and a consequence of this is a steep shoreline. The depth of the wreck site was between eight and eighteen metres.

To produce an accurate record of excavation and the work progress, the area had to be covered with two metre square metal grids, like an empty crossword puzzle. Placing and anchoring the grids was the first problem.

A large barge was anchored over the wreck site. It had been converted for us to use as a dive platform. It had been decked with timber and a set of stairs had been installed at each end, giving access to the immense hold. Cage lockers had been placed in the hold with simple benches. This became a changing room for the divers and general hold all store. A canvas awning was placed over the barge as protection from the sun and occasional rain, and simple wooden garden sheds were placed at each end, providing us with a couple of offices. We had electricity and fresh water on board, brought out by cable and hose from the shore. It gave us a shower to get rid of the salt water and wash dive equipment. The longer we were on board, the more improvements we made.

  We were diving using a surface demand system, which meant pressurised air was pumped through a hose to the diver. We breathed normally through our demand valve regulators. In case of any type of failure in the surface demand system, we carried high-pressure air cylinders on our backs. These could be turned on and used to breathe in the event of an emergency or failure of the surface demand equipment. This would allow the divers to surface safely and under control. The main source of air was a normal industrial construction-type compressor that filled a large reservoir in the hold. The reservoir had air taps connected to it that allowed up to six divers to dive at one time. From the reservoir, the air was fed through a filter and an oil/water trap in to a take off manifold, and the divers' hoses were attached to the manifold. We had a twenty-metre length of air line to each diver. When not in use, the hoses were coiled in a figure of eight and hung on hooks on the metal awning frame. At that time we could not get hold of any pressure couplings that swivelled to put on the hoses, hence the figure of eight. Sometimes, if the diver had done several rotations during his dive, trying to coil the hose was like wrestling a snake.

We did not do dives requiring decompression. A local diving firm owned the re-compression chamber (RCC) in Mombasa, and I did not consider it suitable. There was no facility for giving oxygen, no transfer under pressure (TUP) potential and it had a faulty airlock. We avoided going into decompression stops.

We dived using British military diving tables, with a double safety margin of using the table of the next greatest depth and the next longest bottom time. Therefore, each dive was done within the limits of the dive tables, which, in those days, were extremely safe. During the thousands of dives done on the wreck, we never had one decompression incident.

We were accommodated in the showground on the Nyali Shore. There was a collection of buildings, an arena, water, electricity, hard standing, a kitchen, showers, in fact everything we required. We hired a local cook who provided breakfast and an evening meal. At midday we had a light lunch, usually soup and tropical fruit. It was a paradise. The team was fantastic. Whether by coincidence or design, we were all non smokers. That is quite important to me. There is nothing more selfish than a smoker, and when you live in close proximity to each other it is really offensive, and they continually smell of nicotine. I remember them all to this day with great fondness and affection.

This team still remains my benchmark in life for what an expedition should be like. I have never again reached the same heights of professionalism, enthusiasm and camaraderie with any expedition as I did with those guys.

We adopted a shift system similar to that used by the military in hot climates. We had two teams of six. Team A would start a shift at eight o'clock in the morning until one o'clock in the afternoon. Team B would then take over from one o'clock to six o'clock in the evening. Team B would then do the eight to one shift the next day. At one Team A would do the next two shifts. It worked a treat. We happened upon the shift system after a few days to prevent us over populating the barge at the same time. There was not enough work for all of us all the time and only enough hoses for up to six divers at a time. There were plenty of other tasks to be getting on with.

The grids were taken to the barge and dropped into the water. They then had to be hauled up the slope, position and pegged to the bottom. Geoff Coleman, a bull of a Royal Air Force rigger with the strength of two men, and myself, elected to do this. The grids were dropped on to the seabed in a tangled heap. Once on the bottom we sorted out the tangled heap, a bit like the game Pick a Stick. We then took off our fins and walked the grids one at a time up the slippery slope and placed them where we estimated the correct position to be. There were some twenty or so grids, each measuring four by two metres. They were not so heavy as unwieldy, but Geoff was great to work with, as we were on the same wavelength, and after forty minutes it was job done.

We then exited the water and another pair dived to secure the grids to each other by windlassing with wire. Small plastic yellow tags were then added to the outer grids. They were either numbered or had a letter from the alphabet on. These were positioned using the top left-hand corner of the grid. The top grids were alphabetically labelled A, B, C, D, etc. The vertical grids were numbered 1, 2, 3, 4, etc. This system not only allowed us to refer to the wreck site like a map or crossword, but divers could be briefed by the archaeologists about where to work, i.e., G6, D4, etc. After each dive, the divers filled out a dive record sheet, describing and drawing what they had come across and uncovered during their dive. The record sheets could then be joined together like a big mosaic, giving a large detailed plan of the site. The ship soon started to take shape.

To aid with the excavation we used airlifts, which are long plastic tubes with anchor weights attached. A flow of air from a compressor is supplied into the lower end of the tube, causing the air to race up the tube towards the surface. This causes a water flow and suction at the lower end, just like a Hoover. The diver positioned himself where he could see and control the suction end of the airlift, thus controlling the quantity and amount of silt being moved away. At a later stage we added flexible extensions to the airlifts, which allowed for more precise use of the tool by allowing us to gain access to previously inaccessible corners. If a large object became stuck in the tube, suction stopped. It then filled with air and would usually shoot to the surface. To prevent this we bolted on a hinged rim with a slightly smaller diameter than the tube, and any large debris would block at the entrance but, by quickly operating the hinged handle, could be harmlessly wrenched away and removed by hand to the pile of spoil.

All timbers and artefacts were marked with a numbered plastic tag, brought up to the surface and kept in fresh water. Of course, all this would be recorded in the dive records and every artefact could be tracked back to where it was found. The soaking in fresh water washed out the corrosive salt. Porcelain and crockery were relatively simple to preserve. Timber was much more difficult as it had absorbed the seawater, sometimes to such a degree that it had become spongy. In those days it was treated with a chemical called polyethylene glycol (PEG). The polythethylene glycol replaced the saltwater and, when dried out, gave the timber a stable consistency.

The diving barge anchored in front of Fort Jesus.

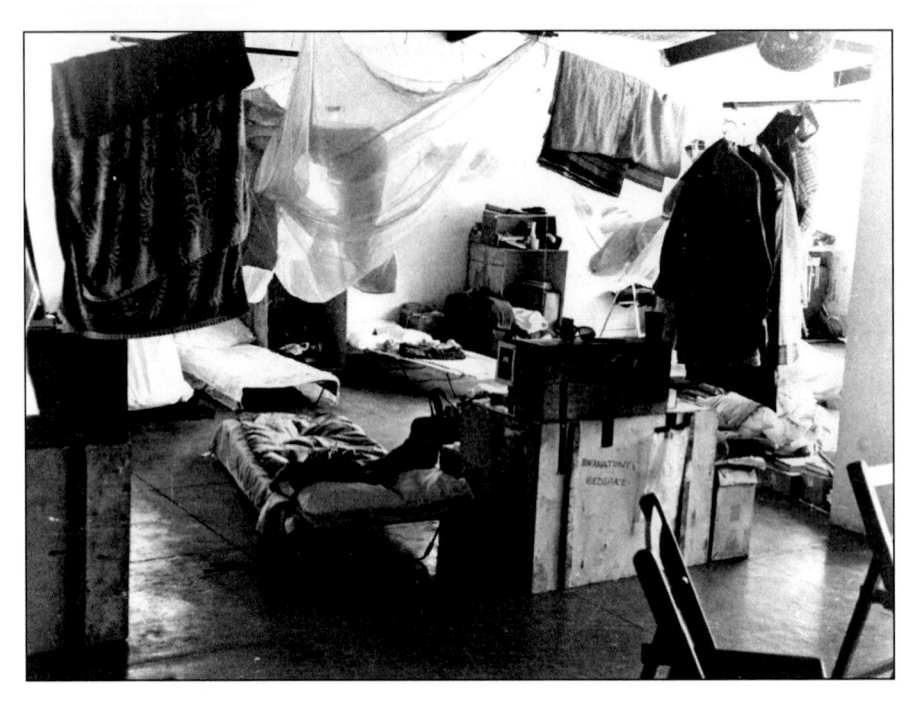

The accommodation in the agricultural show ground, Mombasa.

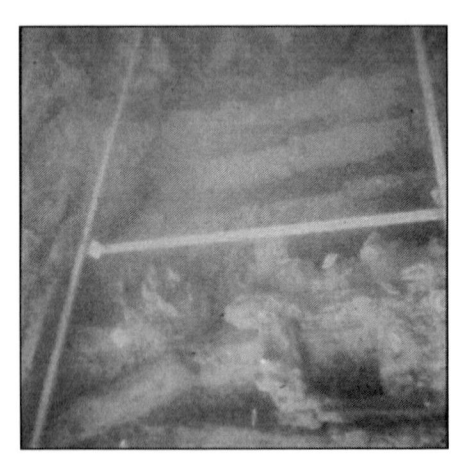

Metal grids 2m x 2m laid over the wreck site.

Diver operating an airlift, note that this usually causes bad visibility.

Diver airlifting using the flexible extension to the air lift, allowing better access to difficult corners.

An elevated view of the site, note Grids, air lifts c/w flexible extensions finds buckets, and a metal basket and buoyancy drum for lifting large heavier finds.

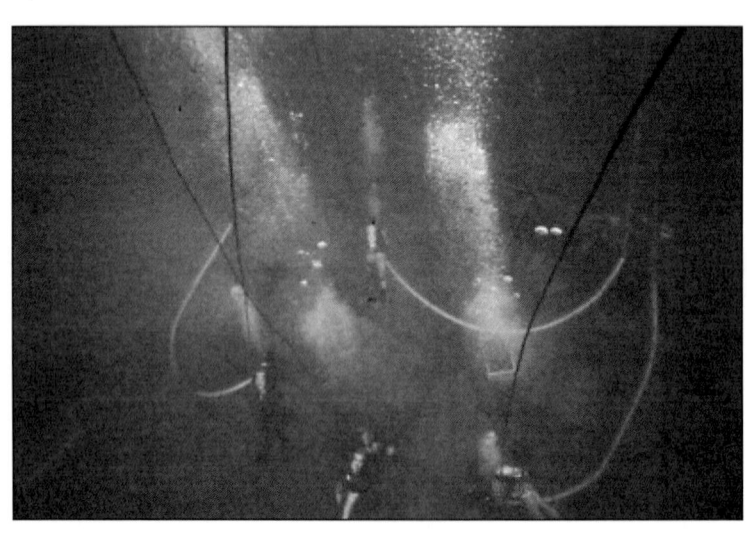

An extraordinary photo of the site from near the surface, showing many divers working on the site. A very rare opportunity due to the water clarity.

Delicate operation of the airlift as the diver is hand fanning the silt into the airlift to avoid sending any fragile items into the tube.

Everything is recorded in situ, here a diver writes his findings and measurements on an underwater slate.

Here divers are using the buoyancy basket to bring things up to the surface.

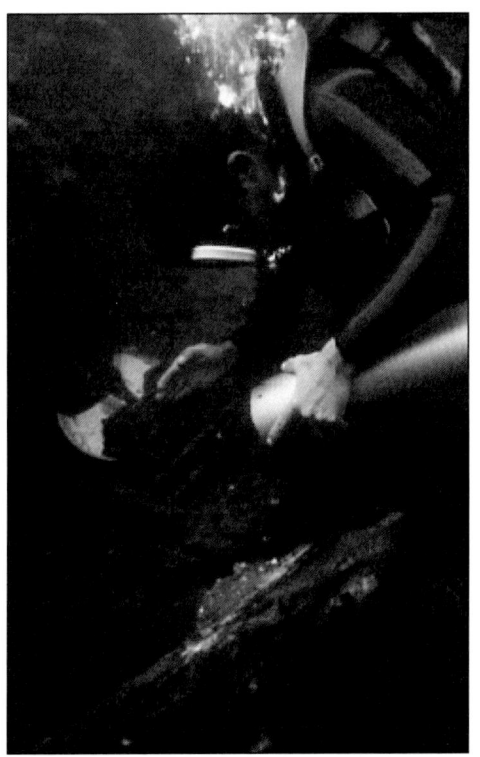

Here a diver is delicately using the air lift to uncover some porcelain.

Ongoing repairs, here a diver repairs a broken air hose which is supplying an air lift.

Artefacts were cleaned, drawn, photographed, recorded, catalogued and preserved. In some cases broken pottery was reconstructed and glued together. A period of friendly rivalry developed between the two shifts, as to who could find the best artefact. I spent almost two weeks just uncovering timbers, which, whilst important to the excavation, did little to boost my standing in the 'finds table of honour'. However, in the grid square adjacent to mine, the diver found bits of porcelain, glass, lathe-turned pieces of wood and pottery. I never heard the end of it. One day I smuggled an old tin plate onto the barge and wrote 'Cowboy's dinner plate, circa 1977' on it in felt tip pen. I hid it under my jacket and descended into my grid. Towards the end of my dive I buried the tin plate in the mud at the top right corner of my grid, which was the top left corner of my neighbours grid. When we changed shifts I casually let it slip that it was a pity my dive had ended when it did, as I believed I was on to something in the top right corner of my grid. I knew very well that my colleague would immediately go down and excavate in that corner. Though I was not there, I was later told that, upon discovering the tin plate, he returned to the surface and reported a pewter find, the first on the wreck thus far. It was deemed so important that two of the archaeologists dived with him and spent some twenty five to thirty minutes meticulously excavating this pewter find. When they eventually got it fully uncovered and read the inscription they were peeved. Spookily enough, they associated the hoax with me, which I thought was a bit unfair, because there were no witnesses. But it was worth taking the flak just to get some revenge.

Apart from the diving, there were many activities to which we could make a contribution, such as conservation and drawing. It was a time of great learning for me, as I also learned to develop and print black white film, and to use an underwater camera.

There was an international aspect to the expedition. Three divers from the Portuguese Navy joined us for a six-week spell. Their arrival coincided with the arrival under the dive barge of a huge shoal of sprats. I often wondered whether they let them out of their suitcases! They joined in the daily routine, spoke excellent English and were good to have along. The Kenyan Navy sent along six divers. These lads had all done the ships divers course with the Royal Navy, so were well versed in lifeline signals and diving procedure. They fitted in well with us, and called me CD1 (Clearance Diver First Class), which I was not, but it is my equivalent in the Navy. They were in superb shape and looked like ebony statues. They each excelled at some sport or other. One of them, Adam Chippa, entered the military boxing competition and won the Combined Service Light-Heavyweight Championship with consummate ease whilst attending his diving course in England. I am envious of such seemingly natural and casual talent.

Some of the Kenyan Navy divers who joined the team. They had all attended the 'Ships Divers' course with the Royal Navy.

Some of the team relax in the accommodation.

After dives we were usually debriefed as here by the AINA archaeologist Robin Piercey.

The excavation team check an assortment of artefacts on the barge deck which were recovered from the wreck site

Après-dive activities in the area were numerous and varied. There was much to see and do. Elevated across the then Kilindini Road, which was the main route to and from the docks, were two sets of huge tusks that spanned the carriageways. It was known as the gateway to Africa. The night life in Mombasa is legendary. The many hotels, on both the north and south coast, always had something going on in the evenings. There was a club for deep-sea fishing and a couple of game parks were within easy reach. The local expatriate community welcomed us to their ranks. They had the Little Theatre Club, which, as the name indicates, held amateur dramatic shows.

One of my favourite clubs was next to Fort Jesus and overlooked the wreck site. The Mombasa Club was an old colonial club with large public rooms opening onto a large veranda with a mahogany railing. It would catch the sea breeze and had a magnificent view over the Indian Ocean and the Nyali shoreline. You could read English newspapers that were only two days old, and a three course dinner on the veranda underneath the swaying palms was ten Kenya shillings. We all became members. It was like turning the clock back several decades. The club had a saltwater swimming pool on the shoreline. A great favourite at lunchtime was a club sandwich and a glass of home made lemonade. That was living.

My main outlet, when wishing to get away, was to the north. A great character called Tony Pape ran the showground. Tony was a Londoner who sold up in the early 1930s and moved to Kenya. He was one of the original white settlers. He bought a six thousand-acre plot of land in the Aberdares, a fertile area up country past Nairobi. I could write a separate book on Tony and his dynasty. Within a short time in the Aberdares he had built his own house. He owned a village, and provided it with a school, hospital and police force. He had to cull some forests of red cedar to make way for cattle grazing. The cedar was of such good quality that he imported a steam driven saw mill from England and started to produce his own cedar. Within a year he had eleven sawmills, all imported and all steam driven. Today the Kenyan houses of Parliament are lined with red cedar, given as a gift from Tony to Jomo Kenyatta, the then president of Kenya.

Everything Tony ate at his table was produced on his farm. Imagine that; tea, coffee, salt, pepper, milk, cheese, water, fruit, all meat, vegetables and bread. It was mind-boggling. In the 1960s there was an enforced policy of land repatriation and Tony bought a one hundred acre plot of Indian Ocean coastline north of Mombasa with its own beach and built a house. That was where he lived. He was seventy (ish) at that time, very lucid, alert and funny. He was also a double for Sid James, the Carry-On comedian. He invited me to stay with him and life got much better. Tony was full of stories and tales of daring-do about the old Africa that would fill a book on their own. He was an amazing character, as was his son, also Tony, so we were the ideal group for anyone with a short memory span. We became like father and son and I loved him very much. Only a few people in my life have been as influential as Tony, and I am proud to have known him.

We would sit on his veranda and look across his lawn through the bougainvillea, frangipani, swaying palms and a large baobab to the sea. We sat and talked in to the small hours. In the morning his cook would prepare a full English breakfast, taken on the veranda. If Tony had to go anywhere I was his chauffeur. I got to know the area well through Tony, and he helped as I tried to improve my Swahili.

Meanwhile, the excavation was progressing well and we had started to uncover large timbers.

I feel that I must tell more about Geoff Coleman. Sitting each evening around the dinner table, it was common for us all to chew the fat. Geoff was stationed in Malta at the time, along with Al Smith who was the expedition photographer. Al told us that Geoff would go octopus hunting off Malta. He would reach into a hole with his head and shoulders inside and come out with a large octopus, up to two metres long from head to end of tentacle. This octopus would wind a tentacle around his head, dislodge his mask and cling on to him. He told us that Geoff would gradually free it and, grabbing its head, would start to move his arm in a large figure of eight so that the octopus would trail after the captive hand and become disorientated. Geoff would then hold out a large goody bag with his free hand and, holding the octopus in front of the bag, would release it for it to swim at speed into the bag. I never saw this myself so I thought he used a good percentage of artistic license. However, I can vouch for the following story. Geoff was a redhead who suffered badly with the sun. He grew a beard whilst in Mombasa and resembled an unkempt Rasputin. He had acquired a large straw hat that he wore as protection. He had a laugh that could stop the traffic and a Geordie accent.

He became a good friend of Mick Hughes, a Navy mechanic. They were both as strong as oxen and rarely ventured further than the small showground bar for their cold beer. Mick was from Northern Ireland and used to dive there with a small, sharpened metal arrow. The metal arrow had a piece of thick rubber bungee attached to its end and a loop. The idea was to attach the loop around the wrist then, by holding the arrow in your hand, you could draw it back under tension. When you released the arrow it would shoot forwards with force, like a bolt from a crossbow. Geoff wanted to have a go. To give you some idea of the strength of these two, they could get metal bottle tops and place them between the fingers of an outstretched hand and then simply close their fingers and crush the bottle tops like a hydraulic ram. On a good day, with the wind behind me, I can only just manage it by using two hands.

The Joint Services Diving Team, MOMBASA Wreck Excavation, 1976 Standing; Eddie Clamp; Nigel White; Alec Tilley; Tim Caldicott; Geoff Coleman; Sitting; Mick Hughes; John Griffiths; Alan Ashworth: Tony Parker; John Weedon; Kneeling; Tony Liddicoat; Alan Smith;

So, armed with the wrist sling, we went off to the reef on our day off . Whilst swimming along enjoying the sights, we came across a moray eel in a hole with just its fox-like head showing. Geoff teased it a little out of its hole and fired the arrow through its body behind its head. The eel immediately shot out of the hole, mouth agape, to try and bite Geoff in the face. It did not quite make it, as he held on to both ends of the arrow like handle bars, and kept the eel off . The eel's body was the size of a large industrial, acetylene cylinder. It squirmed and wrapped itself around his head, still trying to bite him. They both fell backwards into the white sand and disappeared in a cloud. Every so often they reappeared, still in a fight to the death. Suddenly they disturbed a small crustacean. Geoff released one of his hands from the arrow, picked up the crustacean and put it into his goody bag. He then gripped the arrow again and carried on the fight.

It was unbelievable. We took the eel back to the barge and hung it up to skin and prepare it for cooking. It was two metres and twenty centimetres long and was delicious. I was quite astounded and said to Geoff 'What the hell were you doing, letting go to pick up that tiny prawn?' He said 'Ye cannae let them go. They're canny eating.' After that I believed all the octopus stories and thought that perhaps they were even played down. I remember Geoff with fondness, not only for his humour, but he was probably the most fearless and amongst the strongest divers I have ever met and dived with.

Two other members of the expedition, Alan Ashworth and John Weedon, were instructors at the Joint Service Diving Centre at Bovisand, Devon. John Griffiths was the local procurement man and Nigel White was the medic. Nigel was an Italian-looking smoothie who broke lots of hearts when we finally had to leave at the end of the expedition. The diarist was Eddie Clamp, a super guy who I met later on the Mary Rose project. He is the only one I still contact regularly. Tony Parker was the only other army diver and a trained draughtsman. Tim Caldecott, who joined the navy in his youth as a stoker, completed the team. Tim was multi-talented, as they all were, and scooped a bonanza in front of us all when he laid a card on the table at Buckingham Palace with all our signatures on and left his pen alongside. Prince Charles, the patron of the expedition, was looking along the display of photographs and memorabilia and picked up Tim's pen to add his signature to ours. It is probably a family heirloom now.

The expedition leader was Alec Tilley, who I mentioned earlier. He kept us all on an even keel and never stifled or micro-managed us. He was exactly what we wanted. Each member of the team was different, but excellent at what they did. The excavation was seasonal due to the arrival of the monsoon season, so work had to stop. In our first four months we had excavated down approximately two and a half metres in places and had recovered several thousand artefacts. Whilst the monsoons stopped us from diving, the conservation process could continue and did for several months. Our last task as divers was to cover the wreck site with silt to protect it from erosion and looting. The intention was to reopen the excavation at a later date. We used the airlifts to refill the site and it was job done. We flew back to the United Kingdom on the eleventh of April 1977.

We all met up again in London. I received a call from Alec Tilley who said that Prince Charles wanted to meet the expedition members and hear about the expedition, so I went to London and was accommodated in the guards sergeants mess. I bought a suit and pair of shoes (which were crippling after five minutes), and we had a fabulous afternoon in the palace. We were in one of the cinemas (there are three), and laid out a presentation of photographs and drawings. I gave an audio-visual presentation about the diving and everyone else took their part. We had tea and sandwiches with the crusts cut off . Tim Caldecott acquired Prince Charles' autograph and afterwards we went out on the town. It was a very emotional night for me, and the last time we were together as a team. I was proud to have known and dived with them all.

The team meet outside Buckingham Palace to give a presentation to HRH Prince Charles.

182

Berlin, The Return

It was back to my day job of being a troop sergeant and running the diving team. I was stationed in the Berlin district of Spandau. The barracks were alongside Spandau prison, which housed Rudolf Hess in those days. There were lots of places to dive and fantastic training facilities. The army headquarters was in the old Hindenburg University of Sport, and the facilities from the 1936 Olympics were still there and in use. I was still swimming, playing water polo competitively and a member of the football team. I had assembled a set of slides from the Mombasa expedition showing the history of the wreck and the underwater progress of the excavation. I was in demand to give the audio-visual presentation to interested parties. I did not mind because, in a small way, I was sharing the experience with others. I became a member of the Army's team of lecturers and spent many evenings from then on giving the presentation to colleges, universities, wives clubs, etc. A quite extraordinary coincidence was hearing that Eddie Clamp, the naval scribe and diarist from Mombasa, had been posted to Berlin and was living at RAF Gatow.

This was a mystery to me, as there was not a frigate or destroyer for hundreds of miles. I went to meet him at RAF Gatow sergeants mess. Two days later I gave the slide presentation to the German volunteer rescue service (DLRG) in Berlin. The preceding month, Thor Heyerdahl (of Kon Tiki fame) had given them a presentation. I was in good company. I gave the presentation in German, perhaps not flawless German, but it was well received. Eddie however, never understood a word, but he liked the pictures.

Berlin was, at the time, very much a place with a live-for-today attitude. It was also like living in a fishbowl. It was geographically in the middle of communist east Europe. The inhabitants were visibly poor, drab and colourless. It was depressing, and much had stayed as it was at the end of the war. It was common to see building facades peppered with bullet holes.

There were many places to dive in Berlin. There are active systems of waterways, canals, rivers and lakes. At some points the east-west border passed directly through the middle of a waterway. When diving in such places we had to make sure we had our military identity cards with us under our dry suits in case we strayed over the border, were arrested and charged as spies. It was a fascinating time in a fascinating city. I did a study of the city and its history. It has more churches than Rome and more bridges than Venice.

In the diving store we had a brand new three phase Draeger compressor. We were the only team that had such a luxury, another example of the economic gulf between east and west. The diving team was used mainly to recover lost stores and for reconnaissance of potential crossing sites. We did some enjoyable dives along the lakeside beaches. On one occasion I found a wallet with twenty marks in it, and under one of the huge bridges in Spandau I found an UZI sub-machine gun complete with magazine, and a cash box. There was never a dull moment in Berlin. As it was classed as an exotic posting, we only did our two years there and no more. Almost two years to the day after arriving there, I was posted to Osnabruck in what was then West Germany.

"Mutual scratching". The neck entry avon drysuit was a good suit for cold water but you could not get in to it unaided, here we see three of us completing the sealing of the neck by clamping the non magnetic bands and neck seal on. (We used to have competitions during 'Op Awkward' to see who could dress in the fastest time, my record was 11 seconds but I heard of a guy who did it in 9.5 seconds.) Note the suit inflation cylinders 'SIU'.

Osnabruck, Holland, Kiel

It was a busy time for me. I took over as troop sergeant of a troop of heavy plant machines and ran the diving team. A regular diving team task was carrying out aptitude tests for potential divers wishing to do the Army Basic Course at Marchwood. We gave them a short dive in the army equipment to give them the psychological experience of diving in black, cold water to see if they could handle it before using up a flight ticket and place on a course. Osnabruck is situated in northern Germany, but too far from the sea to be able to regularly drive in the briny, so local lakes were used.

The sports diving medium in Germany is the German life saving institution (DLRG) and I sought them out. I joined the local garrison subaqua club and became the diving officer. I met a local German diver called Claus Peter Stoll, nicknamed Olly, and we became good diving buddies. Olly was a freelance journalist who wrote articles for the German diving magazine Taucher (Diver) and was their technical officer. He tested and reported on new diving equipment in their monthly magazine. He was a great contact for local dive sites and a good dive partner. He introduced me to an inland dive site known as the Buddenkuhle, which was some twenty miles from Osnabruck. The Buddenkuhle was originally a sandpit that was formed as sand was extracted and used to construct the nearby autobahn (motorway). The sandpit then filled with water and became a campsite for locals. It had a sandy beach and swimming area. It also provided good diving and a fishing lake. It was safe for families with young children so Annie, Gary and Sarah often accompanied us on dives, and we would make it a family day out and have a barbecue.

Olly told us about an annual divers' weekend party in Holland at a town called Dreischor, so we had a weekend in Holland diving in the inland saltwater lakes, which are protected by huge dykes. It was relatively safe sea diving, without tides, currents or traffic.

The team went to Holland for the weekend. We used military tents ,vehicles and rations and I usually took the family and our own tent or caravan, Gary and Sarah are inquisitive as always.

A problem began to emerge domestically, in that both Gary and Sarah would watch me jumping into the water and then try to copy me. Annie was frantic whenever she turned her back and one or both of them were gone. On one particular day Sarah vanished and we eventually found her sitting on a bench chatting away to an old Dutch fisherman who probably never understood a word. The priority became teaching them to swim as soon as possible, which we did. At this time I started to give Gary diving lessons (age six) and that became a regular activity for us both. Initially he was on an octopus rig with me, and later I bought him his own equipment. At this stage it was all done in the local swimming pool.

It was around this time that the army started to use a new type of equipment called Aquarius, which involved a decanting reserve system. The kit comprised two cylinders on a backpack, but inverted, so that the pillar valve was located somewhere behind your backside. The diver would enter the water with one cylinder on and the other off. When he felt the air being restricted, indicating that the cylinder was almost empty, he would reach around behind him and open up his full cylinder allowing air to decant into the empty cylinder. Once the decanting had been completed, he would turn off the cylinder and continue his dive. When he ran out of air again, he would decant a second time, signal and exit the water. Of course, the decanting process required full use of your hands, which, when frozen, would be of no use, so neoprene mittens became an issued piece of kit (and about time too). Another problem was using grease on an underwater task.

If your hands were smeary, there was a chance that you would not be able to gain enough purchase to turn the valve on and off. It was like trying to open a screw top jar with soapy hands.

Conversion to the New Aquarius Military Diving Equipment

Once the new kit was in, all divers had to be converted to its use. So off to Kiel I went with my team for the Aquarius conversion. We spent a good week up there. It was always good to get back to Kiel. Whilst we were there, we were given a task in a town called Plön, which is situated in the middle of several large lakes. A windsurfer had decided to go out in a storm, capsized and drowned. When we found and recovered the body, we discovered that, unbelievably, he was wearing rubber gardening type boots.

We continued with the Aquarius conversion, which included servicing and maintenance of the equipment. The new demand valve regulator was single hose, signalling the end of the twin hose system in the forces. Sadly, we still had the suit inflation cylinder. I felt that I had to do something about that, somehow.

Training at Kiel allowed us to use equipment which we did not hold in our units, the Temple cox bolt gun and oxy hydrogen cutting torch were amongst the items we could train on.

The old floating pontoon we use to have had been replaced by a rigid pier with piled legs.(Note that the guy tending a diver at the far end was our driver who we trained as a tender.)

Diver entering the water from the jetty.

Diver using a Divers underwater communication Set, (DUCS)

A sheet of 1 inch thick metal plate which had been cut and then patched underwater in nil visibility. Such training is essential if you wish to remain competent in using the equipment.

Back at Osnabruck we continued diving in the Buddenkuhle and a lake called the Gertrudensee. The Gertrudensee was a disused open mine. There was a railway line with a couple of carriages still on it, an upturned rowing boat (empty) and an assortment of munitions dumped at the end of the war, which made the diving interesting. The Gertrudensee was a big silt trap and clouded up badly during a dive. Therefore, unless you were the first in, it was, quite frankly, a waste of good breathing air. The Buddenkuhle was more diver friendly. At the far side there was a line of sunken trees. These prevented fishermen casting their rods, as they would lose their tackle (ouch!). The strands of hooks and weights dangling from the trees underwater bore witness to this. Lying in ambush amongst the branches were several very large pike. By large, I mean five feet long with the girth of a large air cylinder. One of them was known as Isadora, and was the dominant fish in the lake. There were a couple more that were about three-quarters of her size. Her location would be passed between dive groups as they met on the shore.

There was a frightening incident at the Buddenkuhle, which did not affect me, but I knew the divers involved. It was coming to the end of a long cold winter and there was ice on the water. At the beach, where many divers entered, the ice was glass thin and broke easily as you waded or walked into it.

A couple of German divers had started their dive at the beach and took a compass bearing to the far side, where they planned to exit. They swam across, perhaps two hundred metres then, low on air attempted to surface. They could not break the ice. The far side of the lake was continually shrouded in shadow from large trees and the ice was more than thirty centimetres (twelve inches) thick. It was only because the more experienced of the two took his cylinder off and used it as a battering ram to crash a hole through the ice that they were able to get out safely. They were both below ten bars content when they eventually got out. Phew!

The infamous pike 'Isadora' lying in wait amongst the fallen trees in the Buddenkuhle, a German man made lake.

Mombasa 1979, Phase 2 of the Wreck Excavation

Whilst continuing with my job as troop sergeant and running the diving team, I became aware that the Mombasa wreck I worked on in 1976 was reopening that year. I saw the possibility of taking my own Army team out there, but it would take some selling to my Officer Commanding (OC). I mulled it over, and realised that the period in the year that the excavation would be in progress was also the time of year that the Army used to undertake a construction exercise in Kenya. If the unit going out to do the construction task had a deficit of some tradesmen or skills in a particular trade, then perhaps my unit could provide what they needed. It was a long shot. Before I knocked on the door of my officer commanding for permission to attend the excavation with a diving team of nine men, I decided to sweeten the request by offering to take another twenty men from under his command. Hopefully, he would see what a fantastic opportunity it would be for them to broaden their experience and practice their artisan trades. Additionally, it is the fond memories of such experiences that keep soldiers happy during the less enjoyable winter tasks that would certainly come their way later in the year. Thankfully he saw the point and gave it his blessing.

I formed the diving team, letting it be known that only non-smokers need apply. I started planning and organising stores, freight and flights. The surface demand system has been left out there in 1977 and would continue to be the main diving equipment. Once the team assembled, I took them to Kiel for a pre-expedition training course. Not all of the team was from my unit, as a couple of my divers did not want to go and I knew that, by making it compulsory, I would end up with pressed men. This would have been quite useless to the expedition. You have to want to be there, and the guys I took out all really wanted to go. Upon returning to the Army at the end of the expedition, it is quite common for individuals to be down and out of sorts. Very often, a knee jerk reaction is to apply to leave the army. I made it a spoken rule that no such decision should be made by anyone for six months. This would allow for things to settle in their minds. The heady atmosphere that can be experienced on such a good expedition can cause you to make bad decisions. If they still felt strongly about it six months later, then so be it. They all agreed to this, and of course the same rules applied to me.

On the second of January 1978 we boarded a Royal Air Force VC10 to Nairobi. A couple of weeks before we flew, Annie and I had the news that she was pregnant again. This was unplanned and quite a surprise.

We quickly settled in Mombasa, and I found it was nice to be back. This time our accommodation was on the main island, on the sea front overlooking the wreck site. The Institute of Nautical Archaeology (INA), who were overseeing the excavation and providing the marine archaeologists, had rented a huge Muslim-owned house. It was a catacomb of rooms and stairs. We had our own kitchen, ablutions and bedrooms. On the ground floor there was a large room that we turned into an administrative centre and office. This allowed us to do drawings of artefacts and deskwork, collating all records and finds.

We used the same large barge that we used in the 1976 Joint Service Expedition, which had been positioned for us by the Mombasa Port Authority. Commuting to work each day entailed walking down through the Mombasa Club to the waterfront in shorts, flip-flops and T-Shirt, with a towel slung over our shoulders. Access to the barge was via a raft constructed from oil drums, on which sat a timber deck and handrail. Stretching from the barge to the shore was a cordage rope, which passed through the raft handrail, thus securing the raft to the rope. People wanting access to the barge or shore would get on to the raft and pull themselves across to the required destination. It worked well. The surface demand equipment was shaken out and tested. It was still in good condition, testimony to the close down maintenance and good corrosion preventative packing we had done at the end of the previous expedition. Work began on relaying the grids, placing the airlifts and anchoring them in place.

As we had covered the wreck after the first season with spoil from the airlifts, the first task was to uncover it again to the same level. Using six and four inch airlifts with flexible trunk extensions, we soon achieved this. Once we were down to the depth of excavation required, we adopted the system used previously. Divers worked in the grids and then produced a written and drawn dive report.

The main difference with the wreck was that the timbers were becoming much bigger. We were beginning to reach the large construction timbers, ribs, hanging knees and keelson. Identification of where we were in relation to the ship's construction made the excavation more accurate. We were able to confirm these theories with pertinent finds. For example, you would expect to find more porcelain and crockery in the ship's galley area. By now it was known that the ship was built in Goa, India, from Goan teak. It is a timber that is very resilient to marine boring worms, and was one of the main reasons why the buried timbers were in such a good state of preservation. We came across a large number of ballast stones, which were identified as coming from Goa. The wreck was beginning to make sense and come to life.

The diving team still had a multicultural feel. Divers from the United States of America, Australia, Sweden, Kenya and South Africa joined us. The main spoken language remained English, due mainly to the fact that I was giving the instructions and briefings, and the only language I knew well enough to do this in at the time was English. They were a great bunch of people and fascinating to work with.

We uncovered a large ferrous concretion. It was quite big, and we assumed that it was made from cannonballs that had concreted together. It was approximately two metres long and one and a half metres wide, and was becoming an obstacle to progress. We had to bring it up, but it was much too big to manhandle. It was too heavy to lift by hand or using the small derrick crane on the barge. It was also very brittle, and slinging it with canvas straps would probably cause a weight imbalance, which, in turn, could cause it to crack and break. It was therefore decided to break it up using explosives. These were not the size of the charges mentioned earlier, at Scalpay harbour. This time we would be using tiny one-ounce charges placed in small, natural contour fissures of the concretion. It worked like a dream. The concretion cracked into manageable lumps and could then be lifted to the surface. More than one hundred cannonballs were found in the concretion. To my knowledge it is the first and only time that explosives have been used in archaeology.

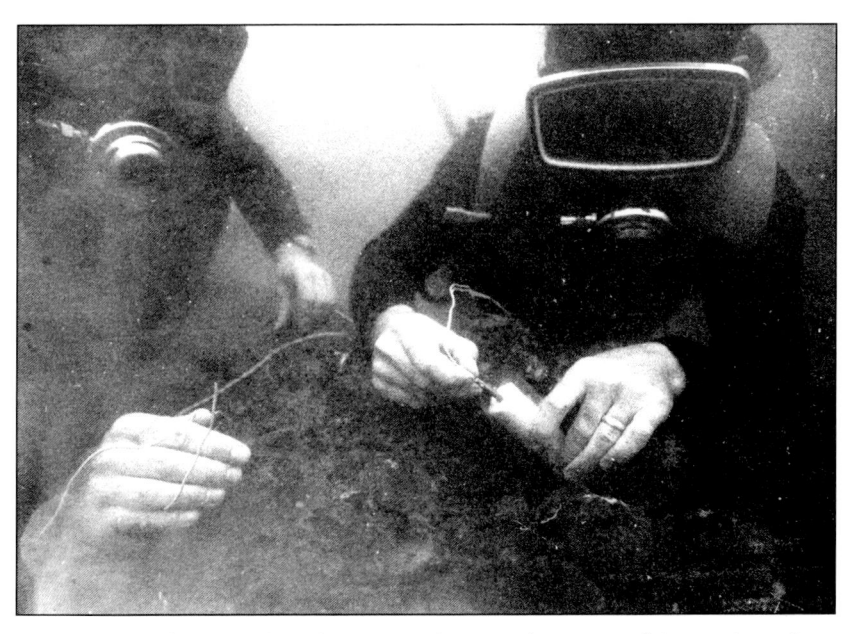

Divers placing the plastic explosive charge and inserting the detonator along a fissure of the large concretion.

Once the concretion was out of the way we were able to continue. The concretion, which weighed well over a ton, had probably been located on the upper part of the ship near the cannons. It had probably, due to its extreme weight and dense mass, moved to the keel area of the ship because of the rotting and disintegrating timbers. I continued to airlift beneath the area of the concretion and found my best ever artefact. I saw it, glistening, bright, shiny and white in the gloom. I carefully excavated it and found that it was a small Ming vase with a lovely blue pattern. It had been made during the reign of K'ang shi (1662-1722).

You may remember that, at the beginning of the whole project, the magnetometer survey had indicated the large deposit of ferrous metal positioned centrally on the wreck site. It was good to eventually find and recover it.

The team of 1979

There was much speculation about whether or not we would find cannons. Records indicated that the wreck lay partly exposed, with a bad list on the surface for a while. It was therefore assumed that every thing deemed useful would have been recovered, salvaged or looted, depending on whom was doing the finding. So far no cannons had been found or recovered from the wreck.

I renewed my friendship with Tony Pape and spent much of my free time at his house on the Indian Ocean. Annie flew out for a couple of weeks with Gary and Sarah. By this time she was four or five months pregnant, and the humidity and heat were very tiring. Tony made them welcome as if they were his own family. I had a week off from the expedition, as everyone had, and we took the opportunity to go to Tsavo game reserve. I drove the car as Tony's driver. Tony had arranged a couple of bandas (simple huts) for us at a place called Kitani through his contacts.

We awoke in the morning to a cloudless dawn and the mighty Kilimanjaro overlooking us. We visited a safari lodge run by a German, Peter Mangwitz. He proved to be quite a character, and when he heard that I had been stationed in Berlin, he became quite homesick. His eyes glazed over and he said, 'Listen Tony. When you get back to Germany please tell them that there are still some Germans here in Africa, holding our positions!' Tony had brought him some sea fish from Mombasa, which was usually hard for him to obtain. The fierce heat usually meant that fish went off before it could be eaten, but Tony had packed it in large boxes full of chopped ice. It was a great experience, and we have never forgotten the safari or Tony's many tales of Kenyan days gone by.

A photo mosaic of the excavated hull timbers of the wreck'.

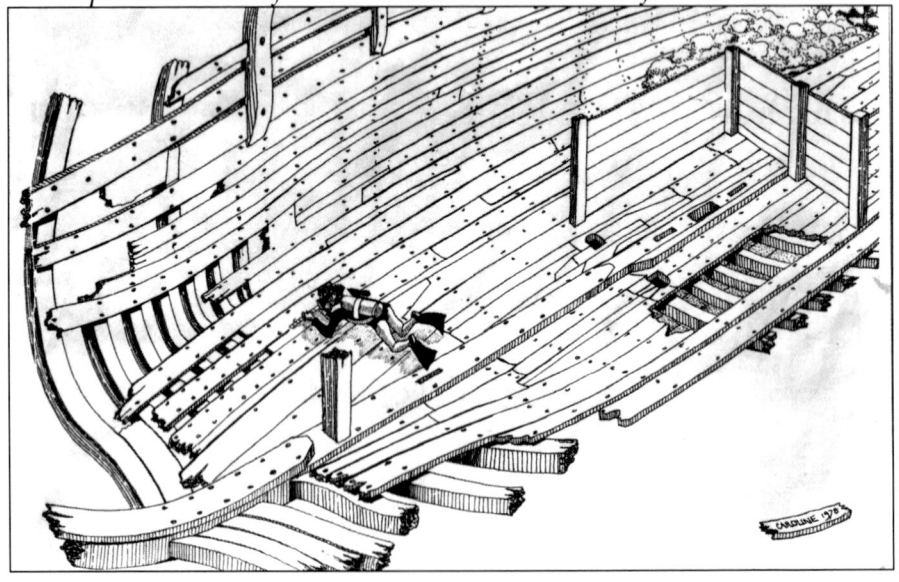

An artists impression of a diver working on the hull timbers of the wreck (drawn by Caroline Sassoon)

One of the final tasks was to carry out a trilateration survey of the wreck. We had excavated the whole area of the hull, and swimming over all the planking, ribs, keelson and frame timbers was quite an experience. The trilateration survey provided us with the ship's lines. I liken it to slicing up a hard-boiled egg. You end up with different sections of sliced egg. It can be held together, retaining its shape, or the individual slices can be studied and then put back together. Every metre or so, you could have the measurements of a slice of the ship, which could then be transferred on to paper by a draughtsman to show the exact shape of the ship.

Two of the divers working together carrying out the trilateration survey of the wreck.

The expedition reached April, and it was time to think about closing down the wreck site before the monsoons and in anticipation of a future season. The re-covering of the wreck with spoil proved to be a mammoth task. We had excavated another couple of metres during the season, which, along with the excavation depth from the previous season, meant that we needed to backfill a depth of up to four metres. It took us eighteen days to complete the backfill. The season over, we bade our farewells. I said goodbye to Tony Pape, who was like a father and best friend to me. I did not realise it at the time, but I would never see him again.

Tony Pape and I sitting on his veranda in his house at Vipingo, north of Mombasa.

Mombasa Summary

Expeditions such as this provided the military with opportunities to get away from a rank- and status-conscious institution, and let the men express themselves in a team where self-discipline, industry and initiative were encouraged. Not performing well meant letting the team down. It built camaraderie and team spirit. To this day, my benchmark for all expeditions remains that Joint Service Expedition of 1977 in Mombasa.

We had responsibilities outside the aims of the expedition. Some isolated places around the world might never have seen or met Europeans before, let alone anyone from England. Therefore, they would form their opinions from our behaviour. It was our responsibility to leave a favourable impression. There are well-publicised examples of expeditions that assembled skilled teams that ruined everything by giving a bad impression of themselves. At this time in my life I have to admit that I was naive.

I had already been to Mombasa and I felt quite involved with the wreck excavation, the people and its aims. I offered to help as best I could with the next season's excavation. Even though I could not attend, I offered to form another group of Army divers to assist with the excavation. I was unavailable because I was on an operational tour.

In order to maintain continuity and for his local knowledge, I chose a person who came out with me on the 1979 expedition. Without going into details, it was a mistake, and I let my friendship cloud my better judgement. He took a prominent role the next season and all did not go well. I was still in touch with some civilian members of the team, and received a detailed account of how things had gone wrong. It still makes me wince when I think about it. There was bad feeling between the archaeologists and the service team.

This individual and the person who was doing my job kept the money given by the military for food and rations for the team. They kept the military donation money for themselves and ostracised the civilians. To add to the shambles, one of them falsified his diving logbook and claimed he was more qualified than he was, touted for a civilian job and got it. He carried out the task in expedition time and kept all the money he received to improve his own lifestyle. However, the worst thing they did as far as I am concerned was to abuse Tony Pape's hospitality. Using my name they sponged off him as much as they could. Tony told me how sick he was of their attitude. It was painful to read.

Shortly afterwards they had the idea of forming a safari business based in Kenya. One of them took out a bank loan, bought a load of second hand tents and trucks, dumped them on Tony Pape's land and started squatting there. Tony wrote to me and explained how fed up he was with it all, but that he was going into hospital for a minor operation and would sort it out when he returned. He died whilst convalescing soon after leaving hospital. The safari business collapsed when the wife of one of the men ran off with all the money and he was left penniless. The trucks and tents had to be towed out of Tony's farm.

I had put a great deal of effort into the Mombasa wreck, yet the Army was never asked back. I write this to reinforce the earlier statement about honouring your responsibilities to your country. Once you get it wrong, it is very difficult to put right. Nowadays I am much wiser about protecting my standards, my boltholes and my friendships, but only after that very brutal lesson in life.

Back to Osnabruck, Germany

After the expedition we returned to normal life in Germany. During the expedition I had been signalled the news that I had been promoted to Staff Sergeant. This meant greater involvement with my new troop and a busier time all round. I continued my role as Diving Officer of the garrison subaqua club and diving with Olly.

The team I took to Mombasa had framed an old sepia print of an early Army diving team and added our signatures to a surrounding border. We assembled outside the office door of the Officer Commanding. We knocked and all entered, to his amusement.

He quickly worked out that we were all divers, and I then presented him with the signed print. I gave our thanks and appreciation to him for letting us go to Mombasa. His name was Spencer Lane-Jones, and to this day I very much appreciate his selflessness in allowing us the opportunity to go to Mombasa.

A humorous incident occurred when I sent a copy of the expedition report to the General Officer Commanding (GOC) at divisional headquarters for his perusal and retention. This was done to satisfy military etiquette. You never really got to know if the reports were read. However, I was given a fairly strong clue when, some time later, I received a reply on divisional headed paper signed by the General Officer Commanding, congratulating me on leading an expedition to Mozambique!

Even though I attempted to make diving enjoyable and get the guys to want to do continuation training, it was very difficult to shake off the bad image of Army diving training and install a sense of fun. Those that went with me to Mombasa were now convinced that diving could be both professional and fun. There was much to be learned from the relative freedom of sports diving, but it was always an uphill task to convince those lads who had endured the hardships of the basic Army course. I began to wonder why the army diving school did not put in a one-day module as an introduction to sport diving. This could prove that there was a fun side to it and therefore encourage lads to take up sport diving. However, in those days there were no takers except me, and as much as I tried to convince people, I was alone and took my fair share of stick for pursuing sports diving in my free time. Almost all the other divers were only in it for the money. I think they were missing out on a great deal. I would later have a chance to do something about it, but it never lasted.

Whilst at Osnabruck I was the 'Diving Officer' of the garrison sub aqua club. When I left the area on posting, they surprised me by giving me this photo of me and Gary doing a beach dive at Kiel.

Vogelsang, Germany

My unit went on exercise to Vogelsang, which was a fantastic training camp on the border between Germany and Belgium. It was built into an area of large hills. It would be an overstatement to call them mountains, but the scenery was quite breathtaking. The training camp had been built between the wars and was purpose-built to train soldiers. The architecture, huge statues and facilities made it second to none as far as I was concerned. It had an indoor swimming pool, ranges for all weapons, large lakes and fitness trails. We were there for a few weeks, and at weekends the divers amongst us took advantage of the superb facilities.

Vogelsang's history of use by the German Wehrmacht meant that you never knew what you might come across underwater. I let slip that the local villagers were talking about a briefcase full of jewels, which was owned by the Gestapo and hurriedly disposed of towards the end of the war in the water at Vogelsang. Of course, I had made it up, but I have to say that I never saw a more motivated bunch of divers in my life. I could hardly get them to leave the water. Sadly the diving was very boring because the big lakes, like all lakes in mountainous areas, acted like silt traps and contained all the top soil from the region that had been washed away. This made for tedious nil-visibility diving. The lake that we dived in was called the Obersee. The divers did not speak to me for a couple of days when they realised that I had been joking.

I had taken up underwater photography as a hobby, and Olly had procured a Nikonos III underwater camera with a tray and flash attachment, which he had given to me. It was most generous of him, as he had acquired it through his job as technical editor for a German diving magazine. Whilst I really enjoyed the activity, my enthusiasm was greater than my talent, and I still have several thousand slides taken underwater to prove this point. However, I gave myself an A for effort and the jury are still out on the assorted results. The problem was that if you decided to do photography, then that was all you could do. It had to dominate your whole dive, and you could not reliably perform any other task. This meant that, at times, the effort, dedication and priority required to take a camera down became a hindrance, especially if there were other things to do. Some years later, I was at one of the annual diving meetings.

There was a programme of presentations. One of them was by a well-known British underwater photographer who gave a presentation on how to achieve the best photographic results. When he came to discussing mistakes and the causes for poor photographs, he said that at this stage he would usually show examples of bad photographs but he did not own any (smart ass!). I put my hand up and said that I could help him out as I have an inexhaustible supply. He saw the funny side. Anything to help out a fellow diver! I was still responsible for maintaining the efficiency and readiness of the unit's diving team. It was now required that all unit teams had to spend a week at Kiel, being assessed by the diving unit there. It was my unit's turn to go, so we packed up the diving store and up we went. It was a two-week course. We carried out a variety of engineering tasks covering most of the likely roles we would be required to perform. We carried out search recovery, construction, buoyancy, cutting, explosives and helicopter jumps if an aircraft was available. We practised our techniques and brushed up and honed our skills. A British yacht club was located in the same small bay and any small maintenance jobs, recovery and checking the bottoms of the yachts were all viewed as mutual scratching. This also gave the divers a thinking job to do instead of wasting good breathing air. Towards the end of the week we had proved ourselves to the satisfaction of the assessors. The buoyancy exercise was done on an old sunken car, and we had a good search day over at an old weapon pit where many weapons and munitions had been dumped at the end of the war. I found a Mauser rifle with its leather sling and magazine still attached. It was in fairly good condition as it had been under a metre or so of mud. It was a trophy I lovingly set about restoring.

Kiel was a fabulous town and not only good for diving, but steeped in history. During the last war it was a large U-boat base and had massive shipyards. There was a huge U-boat pen that allowed submarines to enter and be completely protected from bombing raids by a thick reinforced concrete roof and walls. This had been destroyed after the end of the war but had collapsed and lurched forwards during the explosions, and had not broken up completely. It remained an eyesore, like a row of jagged teeth in the harbour.

A square blockhouse concrete bunker, which sat at the entrance to the submarine pens with an anti-aircraft gun on top of it, had remained intact, but had also lurched forwards, half-submerged in the sea. It was like a fairground crazy house. We used to visit it and try to walk normally but end up crabbing sideways and falling into a corner. You almost had to rock climb or tumble out of control to get where you wanted to go. Many people felt sick at the unbalancing effect that the bunker caused.

It has recently been demolished, but it became a must visit folly to army divers. The army had adopted a new metal underwater cutting torch. For years we had used an oxygen-hydrogen torch called a Sea Fire. The new torch, which was also oxy-hydrogen, was called a Vixen. It was very similar to the Sea Fire, but with a couple of user-friendly modifications. The lads at the diving unit, who were overseeing our assessment, said that we had to test the new torch before we left. It had only just arrived and needed proving. It was obviously too much to ask one of the diving unit staff to get themselves into the water, so I got changed and dived from the diving jetty down to the metal work bench placed underwater for divers to practice basic engineering tasks. I found that the torch worked well, very well, and I signed my name in the bench top, 'LIDDICOAT WAS HERE'. I left the water and reported that the torch worked well. I also knew that it would be a couple of months before anyone saw what I had written, as when I had finished with my team, there was a six to eight week break before the next team were due. The graffiti would remain undiscovered until then. I planned to say that it had to be written by someone else who wanted to get me in to trouble. I surely would not have incriminated myself by writing my own name! Unfortunately, several months later, the bench was recovered for maintenance and I was in trouble. My prepared story about not incriminating myself went down the tubes when they told me that the only time a cutting torch had been used on that bench in the last twelve months was by me, testing the new Vixen. Difficult to waffle your way out of that!

We returned to the unit in Osnabruck. My main job was still as a troop Staff Sergeant and we were still busy in the unique roll of not being armoured in Germany, but being wheel-based mechanised. This meant that we had no tracked vehicles.

Carrying out aptitude tests for the lads who had applied to attend the Army's basic diving course. This was meant to give them as good an introduction to the equipment and diving as possible. We had black painted masks to prepare them for the reality of Southampton water.

Students do somersaults as confidence training as part of an aptitude test before attending a basic diving course.

The team prepares for a underwater search task in one of the industrial canals in Germany.

It was 1980. I was due a posting and was tentatively waiting to find out where I would be sent. The role of my unit changed and we reformed, losing one of the field troops. The troop to be disbanded was mine. This was quite a shock to me. We had spent a couple of years, including a six-month operational tour, moulding the boys into an efficient team. They were now informed that they were to be disbanded and the lads were to be dealt into other sub units. The Army is not given to sentimentality in any way, shape or form so now, without portfolio, I was made Training Staff Sergeant and kept busy preparing and planning all the exercises for the coming training year. It included another trip to Vogelsang.

There were rumours going around that I was due for a stint as instructor with the Army Diving School at Marchwood. I had mixed feelings about this as there was much chat between the supervisors and some strange tales had come from there. For as long as anyone could remember an individual I shall refer to as POM had controlled army diving. He had made diving his empire and, due mainly to a lack of other candidates, had spent most of his career at the head of Army diving.

Strangely enough, no one had ever seen him in a diving suit, in the water or on a diving course of any kind. However, he was given the appropriate title of Superintendent of Diving (SOD). He was all-powerful and the fact that Marchwood, in Army terms, is an out of the way backwater (no pun intended!)

meant that much happened at the school at Marchwood that was beyond the normal accepted protocol within the military.

We all likened it to a Banana Republic, and POM was the SOD on the throne. He was a man who was known to have his favourites and non-favourites. He blew hot and cold with his moods and it was always difficult to know where you stood. I had been an army diver for about seventeen years by that time and had avoided going to the school as an instructor. Many good lads had ended up leaving the Army during a posting to the school. It was a strange place.

My Officer Commanding approached me and said 'Staff , come and speak'. Once we were alone he said 'Your posting is in. You're off to the diving school.' There was a moment of silence during which he must have sensed something was wrong. He then asked 'Do you want me to stop it?' I replied 'No Sir, I know I'll have to do a tour there sometime, let it stand.' It was a decision made instantly, but one of the most critical mistakes I ever made. The posting was a few months away. I continued at Osnabruck and diving with Olly in the Buddenkuhle lake.

Annie and I began to pack up our little house. Paula had not long been born and we were very busy with the family as well. It was our eighth house move. Another concern was school. It was always a struggle to ensure continuity with the children's education, particularly as they got older.

I enjoyed my last few dives in the Buddenkuhle. It was a good summer and I got to know the lake well underwater. Olly had prepared a scrapbook of our various dives together: Holland, Buddenkuhle, Kiel, Greven and the Harz.

We had a beer and said farewell in September 1980. I departed Germany for Marchwood. Nothing and no one could have prepared my family and me for what was about to happen.

1980-1982

Posted to the Army Diving School, Marchwood

This is a very difficult part for me to write, but everything that you read is true, supported by documentary evidence.

I arrived in Marchwood following a drama with our family budgerigar on the ferry. I declared the budgie and took it in its cage to my cabin. I was asked by the ship's intercom to report to the information desk. I went along holding the cage like a lantern. They said they would like to keep the cage in the purser's office until we docked. They said that there was not really a problem and that I should collect it before disembarking. When I went to collect it I found a huge padlock woven through the cage door securing it locked. Thankfully they found the key and I left saying I hoped the budgie had not savaged any of the crew.

I reported to the diving school and met up with the other instructors, most of whom I knew. At a diving conference, POM had cornered Annie and me and told us that the Army was forming a new inspectorate. It was to travel to the Army diving teams worldwide and inspect their readiness, documentation and procedures annually. He said he planned for me to be the Senior Non-Commissioned Officer in the team. I arrived expecting to initiate the new team and set things in motion. It was a new post and the numbers in the school were being increased to accommodate the new team. My expectations were short-lived.

I was used to instructing and supervising on the courses. It was basic bread and butter stuff and it was like joining a sausage factory. All of the courses' instruction was a well-proven format. The lesson plans were done, the programmes were prepared and the stores were ready. It was just a matter of picking up the programme, and continuing and maintaining the work. It was quite easy. Since my early days in 1966, the diving school had been rebuilt. There were new classrooms, new changing rooms, offices and a luxury diving tank with heating, so life was easier all round and more efficient for the staff. On the basic course a week was spent in Wyke Regis, Weymouth. The men learned fast water search techniques using the tidal inlet known as the Fleet, between the land and Chesil beach. It was ideal for the purpose.

Weymouth is another nice town. I had lived in the area during my time as a civilian diver, whilst working in the Winfrith Nuclear Reactor and it was where we recovered the Wessex Mark V helicopter in the sea just off Chesil Beach. It was a lovely town that retained its old Victorian charm, right down to a Punch and Judy show and donkeys on the beach. I considered it a missed opportunity by the Army not to include an enjoyable diving module in the basic course, to show the students that diving could be fun. However, they had not done so, although the courses run at this time were not quite as brutal or miserable as they had been in my time. This was mainly due to the improved facilities. Sadly, students still left the course with a fairly low opinion of diving in general and viewed it simply as a way of earning more money. We could have sown the seeds for a far more fertile involvement with diving, and we were missing a golden opportunity there. During the weeklong course at Weymouth I looked hard at the programme to see where I could procure just half a day to give the students a memorable dive. I managed it by reducing the commuting time to Weymouth. We loaded the kit the day before departure, left earlier and arrived with time in hand. We did the same on the return journey and I had gained us well over half a day. With this newly found time, I worked a fun dive into the week. They still did the whole syllabus as per the programme, but I would take them for a marked swim in an area of decent underwater visibility for a truffle hunt. They all contributed to a kitty, perhaps fifty pence each, and whoever, in my opinion, found the most interesting item collected the pot. I also tried to catch a crab or lobster, and would show them back at the camp how to clean, cook and prepare it. This was something every diver should know.

The idea was very well received by the men. You could sell tickets to hear some of the tales and war stories from this venture.

This activity was unofficial and all the participants were sworn to secrecy. I managed it with all of the courses that I ran. Many years later I bumped in to a guy who had attended one of these courses (I could not remember him), and he said that it was the most memorable day of the whole course. He told me that he was now also a sports diver as well as an Army diver. The feedback I received from him and many others make me feel good about my decision to do it.

There were some new temporary office buildings being lifted in to the camp. This indicated there was still hope that the inspectorate would emerge to fruition. At this time an officer was posted in who was in charge of the new inspectorate. He immediately took up space in one of the new cabins. I shall refer to him as Captain Bran. Nobody had heard of or served with Bran before. He was quite a chubby individual, which, at the diving school, made him look positively fat, as all others were like racing snakes. I went to introduce myself to him but the office was empty. Lying on the top of a desk was his logbook. In diving circles, the mark of a man's prowess as a diver is his logbook. Diving experience cannot be taught at schools, universities or anywhere else other than underwater. The darker, colder and faster the water, the better the diver. It is the same as everything in life, the harder the apprenticeship, the better the apprentice. There are no short cuts. It is for this reason that those who have been taught in the tropics, and only have experience in the tropics, need to re-prove and qualify in European waters. The only accurate source of stating a diver's competence and experience is his logbook. It is not by listening to him say how good he is, or by listening to other people say how good he is, but by what is written in his logbook. The variety of sites, currents, visibility, tasks, weather, circumstances and depths are the benchmarks by which divers are judged. It makes no difference whether they are military, commercial or recreational divers. Their standing in their peer group can only be governed by their personal experience, and that is recorded in their logbooks.

So, out of curiosity I was looking at Bran's logbook when he re-entered the room. He hastily snatched the logbook from me and said that it was private. I said that, on the contrary, it was an Army diving logbook. Each entry had to be signed and verified by an Army Diving Supervisor (ADS) like myself so, apart from being private, it was an open record of experience. To that end it should be available to all Army Diving Supervisors to read, particularly as they were required to certify the dives. I left him with his logbook. It showed he had twenty-eight hours accumulated dive time. Twenty-two of those were his Basic Course. He was practically a novice. Of course, there was nothing wrong with being a novice; we all have to start somewhere.

I continued with my involvement in the courses, and when I had a few minutes would pop in to see Sam Stanley and wile away the time, whilst picking his brains. He was an absolutely fascinating source of information. When we had a patient in the re-compression chamber undergoing a therapeutic recompression therapy, I would assist Sam whilst chatting to him. He made running the chamber seem effortless and was always alert. He would meticulously check the meals before sending them in via an airlock, ensuring the condiment containers were pre-opened to prevent them from imploding, and pay attention to other minute details. The patients could not have been in better hands. Sam explained that a good tip when delivering a patient into the Pot (recompression chamber) was never to get trapped near the door, because when a patient was in the pot, the person nearest to the door would be ordered in as an attendant. If it was a lengthy therapy, seventy-two hours or so, that person could end up having to cancel wedding plans until the treatment was completed. My advice to all reading this is to feign a war injury and hand over the stretcher before you get to the Pot!

One good thing about being at the school was the chance to brush up on all the old skills and equipment because it was all there. I managed to arrange regular dives in standard helmet equipment, operating the pot and using welding equipment. It was an ideal place, not only to brush up on these skills, but also to try any new kit that had come in. Many of the other instructors had trained as either parachutists or commandos. These were lifestyles that lead to fit individuals. They were attracted to diving mainly for the extra money, as the specialist pay was now very good. They were known as bounty hunters, and if the money stopped, so did the activity. Many were great characters and rogues.

They were very much a law unto themselves and whenever I meet up with them again, they retell stories as if they happened only yesterday.

One tale was of a supervisor's course that went to the Channel Islands to carry out a task. Whilst there, one of the students found an outboard motor at the bottom of the sea. At the time, the Sergeant Major Instructor (SMI) at the school was our old favourite AA, who I mentioned was my first troop sergeant. He had now progressed and was a Big Cheese at the school. His self-importance and pompous nature had grown, and as soon as he heard about the outboard motor find he claimed it as his own on the grounds that he held the highest rank. He started to meticulously pamper the motor, cleaning and flushing it with fresh water, hoping to make some financial profit from it. When they returned to Marchwood after the trip, AA had the outboard motor taken to his own store and locked away with a large piece of chain securing the door. Several days later it was discovered that bolt croppers had been used to cut the chain and the motor was missing. AA went berserk, but there was no sign of the motor and no clues either, just permanent grins on the faces of the Special Forces guys. AA eventually left the army. The next day a treasure map appeared on the notice board in the main office. It showed the Marchwood port area and had a large red cross on it.

The map was used to locate the place indicated by the cross, where the outboard motor was found in a shallow grave, preserved in canvas. No one ever found out who did it and if they did, no one ever told.

Divers training for sewer searches

Canadian Combat Divers Course, 1981

Around this time there was much talk of training with other nations called Interoperability. The Canadian Army engineers had their own divers and held an annual diving course and exercise called Roughish Buoy. The British were offered two places on the course in 1981. A guy called Mick Sheedy and I were chosen to attend. Mick 'The Sheed' was a terrific character and a fellow instructor with me at the school.

Our plan was to catch a Canadian Air Force flight from Gatwick to the base in Germany at Lahr. We were to meet up with the contingent from Germany and fly out across the Canadian continent to Vancouver. It was fascinating. We stayed overnight at a place called Trenton. We continued the next day, leapfrogging across Canada, changing our watch times five times as we changed time zones. We eventually landed in Vancouver and were transported to the main base at Chilliwack. That night, we were accommodated in an off base military hotel called Coqueleeza Lodge, which means something in local Indian dialect, but I forget what. The accommodation was excellent and the food in the restaurant was the best I have ever tasted in any army, ever. The lodge was a couple of miles from the base and, like everywhere when you arrive in the dark, waking up next morning was a surprise. Chilliwack was no exception; but it was the nicest of all surprises. To awaken in British Colombia and see it for the first time is wonderful. Every direction you look is like a magnificent picture postcard with mountains, forests and lakes. It was very beautiful.

I had had some good history with the Canadian engineer divers. Whilst I was at Kiel diving school as an instructor, I took a combat engineer diving course for Canadians who had come up from the Canadian garrison of Lahr. We enjoyed some good diving, with great camaraderie and some fun times. I remember them all to this day with great fondness. I hoped I would get the chance to meet some of them again.

We assembled in the base at Chilliwack and were welcomed by the Canadian Superintendent of Diving (SOD), Major Doug Foreman. He was a big bear of a man with a crushing handshake. The first day was introductions all round. Diving instructors from the Canadian service diving school at Esquimalt on Vancouver Island were also there. They were a great bunch, and the scene was steadily being set for an awesome course, as it proved to be.

The location for much of the local diving was a huge expanse of water called Cultus Lake. It was a beautifully situated inland lake overlooked by mountains and forests. On the opening day we did compass swims on to a vertical buoy line. Hitting a single vertical line was not easy to do whilst finning suspended in the water. My buddy and I swam straight passed it, missing it by six to seven metres after a two hundred metre swim.

We then dived in the Harrison River, which was running at about two knots and quite freezing. However, Sheed and I had brought our Avon dry suits with us. Those days they were still neck entry, so we bought our own spare neck seals and repair kit. The Canadian lads were all using neoprene wetsuits.

The Canadian Combat Divers course assembled at Cultus Lake, Chilliwack, British Columbia

Sheed and I had discussed the problem of the suit inflation cylinder, and the fact that we certainly would not get it recharged during the course. The thought of taking out more than one cylinder seemed ridiculous. I decided to take my own suit inflation hose and operate it from my regulator, which I had been using for years in my sports diving. I thought it was really time to set wheels in motion for getting rid of the suit inflation units (SIU) for good. I casually approached POM and showed him my suit inflation system (for which I did not take credit) to try and suggest that we start to move with the times. I had another idea if we had to use the suit inflation units. We could make up a stirrup adapter that allowed the diver to refill the suit inflation unit by decanting from his own breathing cylinder (their working pressure had been increased to about the same). Whilst this would allow us to fill suit inflation units for courses like the one in Canada in the short term, it did still keep them in use when they should really have been abandoned and replaced. Predictably, POM said that he had had the idea a long time ago and even had a hose and clamp somewhere in a box somewhere in the old stores. Yeah right!

But at least I could now use my suit inflation unit hose in Canada, and if there were any repercussions, I could always say I had discussed it with the Superintendent of Diving before attending the course.

Meanwhile, back on the course, I was on the receiving end of some friendly teasing over missing the buoy line on the compass swim. I told them that we were so far from civilisation that even compasses did not work. It was a great icebreaker. I do not mind when people laugh at me and, hopefully, I will always retain the ability to laugh at myself.

The following days saw us exiting various helicopters with and without diving equipment, which meant we could also take a surface swimmer role. We jumped from Hueys, taking off whilst standing on the skids and then going into a low hover whilst still moving forward. It was exciting and great fun. As we were on the Canadian course we adopted their hand signals. It does not really matter which signals are used providing everyone uses the same and understands them. There was a humorous moment when one of the Canadian lads jumped from a helicopter and did not signal.

The okay signal was a single elevated arm with the hand giving a thumbs up sign. The distress signal is an elevated arm waving from side to side. During the debrief the Canadian, Mort, was asked why he did not signal. He replied 'Because I wasn't sure whether I was okay or not', to which somebody made a thumbs up sign and waved it from side to side in front of his face saying 'This is the signal for don't know'. It gave us all a laugh and we immediately adopted this signal to signify anything on the course that was questionable. It became like a secret handshake and we used it in pubs, on dive sites and everywhere else.

    We also practised fast water drop-off and pick-up from a large powerful workboat. We dropped from the stern into the large stern wave, and also rolled from an inflatable craft tied alongside the workboat. We lined up and were despatched in turn by bounce rolling from the outside tube. Some of the guys bounced along the top of the water like a flat stone for some twenty metres. It was exciting and fun. One of the guys wore a pair of cardboard three-D spectacles under his diving mask.

    Apart from a fast water dive in the Harrison River, all of these dives were carried out in the scenic Cultus Lake, so we got to know the lake well. The facilities there were very good. One day was spent jumping from and being recovered by a Chinook helicopter.

    These huge twin rotor machines are one of the biggest helicopters in the military. Then can even land on water and use their rotors to propel them along, but they need to position a stern board on the ramp to stop water coming into the cabin. We were to jump from the tailgate whilst the helicopter was moving forwards. It was like having a carpet pulled out from under your feet. We jumped in pairs, and at the end of the run across the lake all the divers were stretched out in two lines. We were instructed to position ourselves about four metres apart for the recovery, and the aircraft swung around and realigned itself to pick us up. The pickup was a method that was being trialled. Two eight-metre rope ladders were dangled from the rear ramp and the aircraft then moved forwards through the middle of the two lines of swimmers.

Preparing to exit from the stern of a 'Chinook' helicopter.

The theory was that each diver would grab the ladder on their side and climbed up it and over the ramp. There was severe turbulence from the rotors and the ladders were flailing around. I knew from past experience that, for any work with helicopters on water, a facemask is essential or the spray from the rotor turbulence hits you in the face like high-pressure gravel, blinding you. I advised the Sheed to put on his mask, but he was worried that it might become dislodged and come off in the fall. I suggested that he put it up his arm so that it fitted snugly over his elbow, then place it over his head whilst waiting for the pick up. The aircraft passed over head and I bided my time. I knew that I would only get one chance to grab the ladder. I managed it and immediately felt myself being pulled through the water by the aircraft. I started climbing because I knew that I had to be clear of the bottom of the ladder by the time it reached the next diver in the line. As soon as I was clear of the water, I realised that attempting to climb the ladder in the normal fashion would result in the weight of my feet pushing the ladder away from my body at ninety degrees. I grabbed on to the side and placed a foot on either side of the ladder. This got me to the ramp of the aircraft and then I had all the fun of climbing an overhang, like rock climbing.

I made it and sat on one of the rows of canvas seats, watching the others attempting to get themselves into the aircraft. The lake was littered with divers in the water who had missed the ladder. I looked around the aircraft, no Sheed. I thought 'Come on Sheed', but the aircraft was near the end of its recovery run then banked slightly to port, so I knew it was the end and he was going back to the landing zone. I really wanted Sheed to make it, as we were a good team, the only Brits on the course and conscious of at least holding our own. Suddenly a hand appeared on the ramp, then a shoulder and up popped Sheed over the ramp. His face was behind his arm and he looked at me and gave the 'I don't know if I'm okay or not' sign by waving his thumbs up in front of his facemask. Everyone in the aircraft fell about laughing. Sheed could have needed a hand to get in but we were all too helpless. Well done the Sheed.

Preparing to do fast water drop off's

Divers are launched two at a time from the stern of the boat'

Another method of fast water drop off meant bouncing of a boat tube whilst attached to the fast workboat. The workboat would travel up to 25 knots. We achieved drop off rates of a diver each second. It was great fun.

One of the Canadian divers who did the whole fast water drop off sequence wearing 3D glasses,!!!!!!! (note, a couple of good buddies of mine, Reb Mckinnon and Dave Armitt.)

Fast water pickup. Divers float in the water with their arm elevated. Crew hold recovery ring from pickup boat in to which diver threads his elevated arm, he is then flicked up into the pick up boat.

Fast water pickup takes timing and effort. We did this with and without wearing diving equipment. Note it requires timing, precision and strength to master this technique

*Loading up divers to be dropped By 'Huey'.
They sit in the doorway whilst standing on the skids.*

The 'huey' drops the divers at the drop off point. It flies slowly forward and the despatch sequence of the divers is very important to prevent landing on another diver.

We lived at Coqueleeza during our stay in Chilliwack and commuted to camp daily. On the route of our evening commute each evening was a pub called the Jolly Miller. This proved to have a huge magnetic pull and we would nearly always pop in for a beer on the way home. Everyone would be in uniform, which was new for the British. Walking out in the United Kingdom in any type of uniform and announcing that you are in the military is banned, but on the other side of the world there seemed to be no problem. After an exciting day it was great to relax and talk of old war stories with the crowd. At the weekends we managed to get as far as Chilliwack town and experience some old Canadian culture. A much talked about centre for entertainment where Sheed and I were taken was the Empress Hotel. We had heard about its reputation before we had even left

Germany. It was popular with the local indigenous Canadians (I forget to which tribe they belonged, sorry), and at weekends there was much feasting, dancing and settling of old scores. When enough alcohol had been consumed it would be seconds out and in its recent history tomahawks had even been used along with other weapons. Sometimes the Empress got quite crazy. The guys had given it the comical nickname Moccasin Square Gardens. It was a local curio that had to be visited, and the others on the course ensured that Sheed and I saw all that there was to see.

I bumped in to a couple of the lads who had taken the Combat Divers Course with me at Kiel. One of them, Bob Fiddler, was a renowned and accomplished ice hockey player and had settled in Chilliwack at the end of his career. The other was Paul Johnstone. They had heard that I was on the course and their hospitality was wonderful. I was invited out to dinner almost every evening, which I could not accept because of course commitments. However, it shows the depth of long lasting camaraderie that exists between divers. We are not very good at writing letters but we place camaraderie very high. It was fantastic to see them all again. The course had two phases. When we had completed the Cultus Lake training we spent the second phase at the Canadian Joint Services Diving Unit at Esquimalt on Vancouver Island, Fleet Diving Unit Pacific (FDUP).

To get to Vancouver Island we took perhaps the most scenic ferry boat ride in the world, through a mass of rocky islands with pine trees and small beaches. Our destination was Victoria, the capital of Vancouver Island. The waters were crystal clear, and as I am keen to dive in all of the world's oceans, I was pleased to have my first experience of the Pacific. The facilities were great, the sea life was amazing and the edible crabs were huge. On the diving jetty was a fifty-gallon oil drum full of fresh water and a steam pistol. We used to put the edible crabs in the drum, cook and eat them. Seafood does not get any fresher, but the fact that they had made the effort to install a crab boiler on the jetty proved that they had got their priorities right. Due to the clarity of the water, the sea life was beautiful and unpolluted. I was told that there were times during the year when all divers were removed from the water due to Orca killer whales migrating through the sound.

Another underwater exercise we took part in was practising the removal of a body from a sunken armoured vehicle, which was permanently positioned on the bottom. One of the supervisors would position a life-size dummy somewhere in the vehicle and we would dive in turn, locate and recover him. We carried out a day's explosive training using Canadian explosives. They had a flexible hose explosive that I had not seen before. It was ideal for following natural cracks in rocky features that you were trying to remove. We dived from a craft called a Rotork Sea Truck, which had a ramp bow that could be lowered into the water for ease of diver exit and entry. I took some underwater photographs of the explosives being placed and the detonating ring main being laid. We were hosted generously by our Canadian friends, and the course proved interesting and worthwhile as well as being very enjoyable. It ended with us exiting helicopters into the sea at night, swimming to an inland bridge using compass bearings (I followed somebody else!), placing explosives and being recovered again out at sea. The following evening at a 'ceremony' in a local bar, Sheed and I were presented with our Combat Divers badges. I wore mine with my British uniform until the day I left the Army, and I was very proud to do so.

Preparing and placing explosives on underwater obstacles.

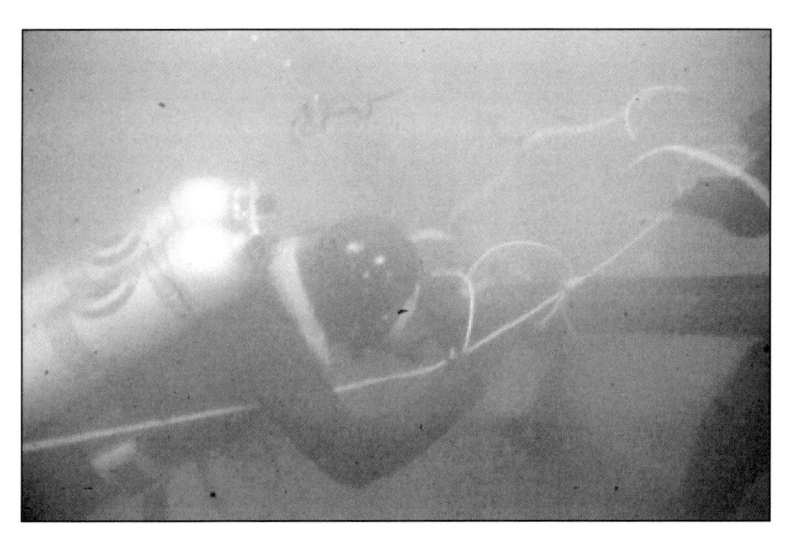

Preparing and placing explosives on underwater obstacles.

The explosives detonating.

The unusual surface demand equipment used at Esquimalt for the search of bodies in confined spaces, there is no bale out cylinder allowing easier access.

The Course assembled at the Fleet Diving Unit Pacific, Esquimalt, Vancouver Island.

We had a few days left before our flight home. Doug Foreman asked us what we would like to do, giving us various options, which included him giving us the keys to his flat in

Toronto to use if we wished. Sheed and I decided to go skiing at a place called Mount Vernon. The skiing was for ten days, which would mean us arriving late back in England. Doug Foreman never batted an eyelid. He signalled the diving school at Marchwood, 'Liddicoat and Sheedy detained for winter warfare indoctrination course. Back to you five days later than planned'. He then sent us skiing. Whilst this book is really about my diving life, anyone who has been skiing will appreciate the beauty and wonderful landscape of the Rockies. If I ever get to write a book about skiing, that ten days on Mount Vernon will have priority. Sheed and I arrived back in England and made our way back to the diving school. It was back to reality. Part of my remit was to give an illustrated talk on Canadian Military Diving, which I did. I also gave a similar presentation on British military diving to the Combat Divers Course. These were small returns for a wonderful six weeks of my life.

The Mary Rose Project, Part 1

On our return we immediately became involved in preparations for the Mary Rose project. The Mary Rose was Henry VIII's flagship, which sank in the Solent. During the sixteenth century it had been partially excavated, and again in the eighteenth century using Siebe Gorman standard diving equipment, which was used by Army divers who were the forerunners of the present day diving school. A team of archaeologists and volunteers had been excavating the wreck for many months and were nearing the completion stage. Most of the ship's timbers had now been uncovered, and there were discussions about raising and preserving the hull as an exhibit. Due to my experience from my involvement with the Mombasa Wreck, I was included in the initial team to go and work on the wreck. It was March 1981, and the weather was not very kind to us. It was mainly cloudy, rainy and there was a permanent choppy swell. One good point was that one of the existing team of dedicated volunteers was Eddie Clamp, a great old buddy who was with me on the Mombasa Wreck in 1976 and again in Berlin. It was good to see him again.

I must add, and it is now an accepted fact, that the Army approached the task in wholly the wrong way. The subject of practical archaeology requires dedication, skill and an attitude of wanting to be there. I tried to explain this to POM, but he was not interested. He just assigned one of the courses to the task, and included a few supervisors from the school. They were good guys but had no desire to be there. The result was friction between the groups. I could see this happening and I gave a quiet word of apology to Eddie Clamp, who came from a military background and understood how and why it was happening. To this day, when I have contact with him, I am reluctant to discuss those days. This was partially a result of the Army's harsh attitude towards diving, which I have referred to previously. It is understandable why there is this attitude towards training. Sometimes there are tasks in military diving that require supreme fitness, obedience and discipline. Therefore, the training is designed to prepare divers for these occasions. It is little wonder that hardly any of the men take up recreational diving. When the two ends of the diving spectrum are confined together, as they were on the support vessel Schliepner, the fact that there was little, if any, common ground contributed to disharmony on the project.

Clouds on the Horizon

As I stated earlier, this chapter is very painful for me to write and I have decided to stick only to the facts.

I went to the Navy hospital in Portsmouth for an annual chest xray as part of my diving medical. For some reason, the radiographer wrote 'I would not recommend this man for submarine escape training'. That was all he wrote, and my instant reaction was that I had not or would ever need to do submarine escape training, so the remark was irrelevant. Captain Bran got hold of the x-ray report and suspended me from diving. When I queried this he informed me that, until I had been given the all clear, that was how things would be. When I mentioned that the remark made in the report concerned an activity that I would never do, he looked directly at me and asked me to close the door on my way out.

I thought that this could get seriously out of hand if it was not handled carefully, and I became concerned. Another cause for concern was the apparent lack of support and reassurance from the hierarchy. I knew that, at any time, POM could have been satisfied that I would never have to do submarine escape training and acknowledged me as fit to continue. We had x-rays annually, so it would have made sense to monitor the situation and see if there were any changes or deterioration at my next medical. However, support was not forthcoming.

I then faced the problem that POM was taken ill. Captain Bran took over his chair and there was no progress at all. The x-ray had picked up a benign hamartoma in my lung. They are usually long standing and had certainly been picked up at previous medicals, but thought to be of no significance. Meanwhile, weeks rolled by and I was stuck at the school as a non-diving diving instructor. The whole thing was getting beyond a joke.

On the fifteenth of June 1981 I was sent by the Army's medical authorities to the Western Hospital, Southampton for an appointment with the chief radiologist Dr. Sterling MD, FRCP. By this time I was very worried. X-rays were taken and Dr. Sterling called me in to his office where the x-rays were on a screen to his right.

He looked at me and said 'So, what's wrong with you? Why have you come to see me?' I said, 'Surely it's obvious. I'm a diving instructor who is just about to lose his living because of what's on those x-rays'. He chuckled. 'Absolute nonsense', were his exact words. He wrote the following in the Medical Examinations page in my army diving logbook: 'Full pulmonary function tests all normal. "Trivial" x-ray changes of long standing and of no physiological significance. Fit to dive.' He then added his signature.

I could have kissed the man. My sense of relief was unbelievable. Diving was my life and I thought that he had just saved it. I found myself whistling as I drove back to Marchwood. I told everyone I saw that I had been passed fit to dive. A while later I was summoned by Captain Bran, who opened with 'I hear you've had some sort of medical report?'(A strange question considering that I had been sent to Dr. Sterling by the Army!) I replied 'Yes Sir', and showed him the entry in my logbook. He told me that what was written was irrelevant, as he would only believe the word of a Navy doctor. I looked at him expecting that he was joking. At any time I expected the door to burst open and all my mates to pile in saying 'Hey that got yah worried, Tone, eh?' But it was not a wind up. Captain Bran was deadly serious. I said that the diving school had sent me to Dr. Sterling. If the intention was to ignore what he said, why had they bothered sending me? He did not have an answer.

It became obvious to me that Captain Bran, who I had been told was a bottle-of-whiskey-a-day man, had the knives out for me. I did not know why as I hardly knew him. I went back to the instructors' room and recounted what had just happened. They could not believe it. I was being set up and there was nothing I could do about it, nothing. The next phase of this fast growing farce was that I had to attend a medical at the Royal Navy Physiological Laboratories at Alverstoke. I arrived a bit early and heard two people talking in an adjacent room. I heard the words 'It would be most useful if you could find something else to support the case'. Two men in uniform then stepped out and stopped speaking as soon as they saw me. One of them came over and told me to strip off . I was then subjected to the most rigorous medical I have ever undergone. Hardly a word was spoken. He tested everything. Much of it, to my knowledge, was wholly unconnected with a routine diving medical.

I am not a doctor, but by this stage I had been diving for eighteen or nineteen years and knew diving medicals quite well. He was doing some strange tests on me for the first time ever in my life. When I dared to break the silence and asked why he was doing such and such, he answered 'Just to be sure'. At the end of the examination I got dressed and left without so much as a farewell. It was a most unpleasant experience, but I know that he found nothing that warranted me being disqualified from diving. I did not realise at the time that naval doctors would not, under any circumstances, contradict the opinion of another naval doctor, regardless of ethics, truth or honesty. A doctor explained this to me later in my life.

It seemed that I was doomed. POM was hardly in work by this time because of ill health and the school was being run by his two acolytes, Captain Bran and Captain Bray. Captain Bray was openly disloyal to POM when it was rumoured that POM might not be coming back because of ill health. That is how the dice had rolled for me after eighteen years as an army diver. The first time I needed to be surrounded by good guys, strength and support, there was none. There is no system for redress that works in the Army, not even to this day. I had no wish to go down without a fight and was now certain that I was being set up. I wrote a letter to the general at the head of the Army Diving School. It was returned a few days later, for POM to deal with me. All that it did was enrage him and make him very spiteful.

I wrote the letter because, the previous day, POM had come in to work and I was summoned. He now had to share his office with Captain Bran. POM was in a benevolent mood and finally reassured me that, no matter what, my future was safe and that I would always retain the qualification of Army Diving Supervisor and should not worry. He then went home 'ill'. One hour later I was summoned by Captain Bran who had been sitting at his desk and witnessed the earlier meeting I had with POM The following is totally incredible but true.

Captain Bran said 'The Superintendent of Diving is a sick man and doesn't know what he's saying. You can take it from me, Staff , that you can ignore what he says. You have no future in Army Diving. We aren't expecting him to come back.' It was incredible. The next day, realising that I was being set up, I wrote to the general to inform him exactly what was going on. It made me feel better but of course, it did no good.

Belize, as a Diving Instructor

Incredibly, to get me away from the school, they sent me to Belize to run the diving at the adventurous training centre at St. George's Caye for six weeks. Captain Bran said that I was forbidden to dive out there. I asked why they were sending me. He told me that it was to supervise and instruct sport diving activities. Not that he of course would know, there were some lessons in sport diving that had to be done and proved under water: mask clearing, hand signals and buddy breathing to name a few. He reiterated that I was not allowed to dive. If I was to obey him it was a waste of time sending me. With the old adage 'Since when have we done what were told' in mind, I decided to partake in full diving activities and training during the six weeks. Whilst in Belize I ran more than eighteen Basic Sports Diver courses and instructed the Special Forces on deep diving techniques at the Blue Hole.

I also carried out an underwater rescue operation on an American tourist who had collapsed with spinal bends after carrying out sport diving up the coast. He was near death when he arrived by Puma helicopter at night, in the middle of a tropical storm on the edge of hurricane George. He had been given the last rites three times. I took him off shore and recompressed him under water twice. My actions were recorded by Diver magazine, which was the official diving magazine of the British Sub Aqua Club. They made me their Diver of the Year in 1981 as a result of the rescue.

The Rescue in Belize.

I now come to write about this episode in my life with some reluctance. I have a problem with writing myself up as a hero and have left this chapter as the last article I wrote, which was to be included in the book.

I was going to include the article used by the BSAC's official magazine at the time called 'Diver' which was written by one of their freelance reporters and based on an interview I gave him. and covered most of the relevant facts. However I do not have the publication rights to re-use it without the authors permission and as the author subsequently went on to make himself a great deal of money by selling the story to other publications without my knowledge or permission, then he would most certainly come chasing me for money. The only alternative is for me to write an article myself, but as stated earlier, I do so with reluctance.

I have always believed that at least once in everyone's life, fate or whatever, comes a knocking and you are put in a position of immediacy where whatever you do or whatever decisions you make or actions you take, can have enormous impact on your or other peoples lives. You will have no idea of when, where or in what form the incident will happen. You will also have no idea of how prepared or convenient it is in your own life and circumstances at that time. You will just have to make decisions and take actions then, which can either haunt for the rest of your life, make you a hero, a villain, a coward, a failure, a success, a somebody, or a nobody. Sometimes you can do your best, make decisions or take actions which go horribly wrong and have dire or deadly consequences.

We have all heard of accounts of daring do, of the fellow climber who decides to cut the rope of his dangling buddy, or the parachutist who risks a mid air rescue. In my view there is only one reason to put yourself under such risk, and that is to save life, there can be no other reason, the person who rushes into the burning house to retrieve the TV is not brave, he's an idiot.

We dive a wreck in the channel which has recorded loss of life of some of the passengers, who were safe and well until they decided to go back down below to retrieve their valuables, enough said.

It was Wednesday 5 August 1981. I was a diving instructor at the Army's Adventure Training Centre, situated on St. Georges Cay a few miles from Belize City. The centre had closed down to students and we were carrying out much needed maintenance on all the adventure training equipment. It certainly needed it, the sand, saltwater, continual use and burning sun really took it's toll. Our diving inflatable boat, (a floppy) had developed a puncture in it's bow tube and we were trying to repair and service it.

The maintenance week coincided with the Army Garrisons annual exercise titled "Montezuma's Revenge" which was the reason for the 'no student' week.

It was 1800 hrs, enough was enough of the maintenance and I had decided on a cold beer. It was already pitch black and the sea crashing heavily up the beach, we were in the direct path of hurricane 'George' which was due to hit us within the next 10 hours. The sea was whipped up into a frenzy and the waves crashing up the beach were some 2 meters high. The rustle of the palm leaves now pulled horizontal by the wind and the thud of the odd coconut as it crashed on to the ground having been ripped from the tree were the background noises. Out of the dark a hand touched my shoulder whilst en route to the beach bar, (whilst it was still there!). It was the centres radio operator asking me to come to the radio room as a doctor wanted to speak to me. The doctor and I had a brief conversation along the lines that he had received a patient, an American tourist, who had an attack of 'Bends' up the coast and who had been airlifted to him. There was nothing he could do for him so he was sending him to me to "Take him underwater to 10 feet for 15 minutes". 30 minutes after the message a puma helicopter landed on the volley ball court and the patient was handed over to me.

    He was in a desperate state. He was laid barely conscious on a stretcher, had been given the last rights 3 times. He weighed over 20 stone and was an absolute dead weight on the stretcher. Since the message we had busied ourselves in assembling the kit required for a re-immersion therapeutic treatment. We inflated the boat, started topping up the cylinders and fitted the OBM. Earlier in the evening we had looked at the stormy sea and made a remark along the lines of 'check that sea fellas, anyone who goes out on that needs his head examining'. (Here we were just about to 'go out in that' in pitch blackness).

    The preparation was part of a daily routine with the team and they busied themselves in assembling the kit and followed instructions admirably. I was the only diver there. I questioned those who had accompanied the patient on his earlier dives to ascertain how deep he had been and for how long.

    I found out that he was a very experienced commercial and recreational diver which was a plus. It would be better than having a total novice who would be petrified when he 'came to' at 31 meters suspended in black water and only me to look at!!!!! His wife was present and although distraught she remained lucid and calm. With her and with all the other eye witness accounts, it enabled me to work out a 're-entry' therapy to hopefully save his life.

Whilst nowadays' re-immersion therapy is no longer recommended, at that time both the US Navy Diving Manual and the British military diving manual the BR 2806 included therapeutic re-immersion therapy's. In my small box of diving goodies, which accompany me wherever I go, I kept some underwater chalk. Once I had the table worked out, I wrote it on my fins and also on one of the inflated tubes at the stern of the 'floppy'. I explained to the 2 man crew not to raise or lower any kit down over the written tables as the downline would erase/remove the writing and as I would be down below, I wanted to be sure that the crew topside could read and understand where and when I needed the replacement cylinders to be suspended.

There were two lads in the boat. The boat operator was Hughie McConnell who was a member of the resident infantry battalion and had done a 'Boat Handlers Course' with the Army. The other was a member of the Army PT Corps, a staff sergeant called Vic Butcher. Vic in true PT Corps fashion was a great character and at sometime in the past had done a sport diving course with the BSAC.

Whilst the boat was being loaded, I was giving the two of them a briefing in the howling wind and being drenched by the waves, (lucky I wasn't using a blackboard!!!) It was time to go. We set off into the darkness instantly disappearing from sight into the sea. The patients name was Richard (Dick) Alba, who was now laying on the stretcher in the middle of the boat in his pyjamas and I was dressed in a Bath rugby shirt and trunks.

After a few minutes the boat and equipment was awash and filled with sea water. This made the cylinders and other kit roll around dangerously as they were semi buoyant. I stood on the bows holding on to the painter rope and pointing the direction for Hughie to steer the boat. In the blackness, I could make out the gaps in the reef, indicated by the breaks in continuity of the line of white surf as it crashed onto and over the reef. We passed the reef and headed into the blackness of the open sea.

Miraculously the stretcher maintained its position in the centre of the boat but was underwater with Dick Alba lying wet but with his head above the water.

I estimated that we were some 4-5 miles out and I dropped the anchor on a 50 meter line. The water depth was several hundred meters so the line was vertical in the water, which was just what I wanted. I made ready a lazy shot which was a device used to support exhausted divers, whilst on lengthy decompression stops. It comprised of a triangle of cordage with the base line made rigid, usually done by threading it through a length of pipe on which the diver sat. He could then sit on the pipe and hold on to the two sides of the triangle. The contraption would then be attached to a vertical down line by using a snap hook. We didn't have any pipe for the seat but improvised using a paddle. I quickly got dressed for the water and dropped the 'lazy shot' overboard and held it on the surface. I wrote down lifeline signals on the boat, so they would know when to 'pull up', 'lower', or 'hold'. We dressed the patient in scuba gear and a lifeline around his chest which was tended from the surface. (Hence the basic signals chalked on the boat.) When we came to put a mask on Dick, we found it swimming around the water in the bottom of the boat, with the glass broken, it had been rolled by the cylinders and had smashed. Time was critical so I gave Dick my mask and decided to dive with no mask to get the treatment started. I said to Vic to see if he could see if there was a spare mask in any of the boats 'pockets' and down we went. Once we were down to 10 meters it was nice and quiet and peaceful. We continued down to 31 Meters and hooked on there. I sent the signal to 'hold on' and there we were suspended in hundreds of meters of water in pitch blackness apart from a torch I had brought. 'Lucky Eddy' here had no mask but despite this it soon became obvious that even after a few moments down there, Dick started to improve, his eyes opened and his legs started to move. It was a huge relief.

It was very peaceful down there but I knew that the whole treatment would be very difficult without a mask, especially reading the gauges. I signalled to Dick that I was going up, he was happy about that. I left him the torch in case the 'Bogeyman' came and I went up to the boat. It was still chaos in the storm. Vic had seen the lights of a passing boat and had cracked a red flare. They were running from the storm but found an old snorkelling mask which they gave him, they wished us luck and sped away, it was a huge stroke of good luck. I donned the mask and returned underwater. As I descended I got a fit of the giggles at the sight of the guys in the boat who were now up to their knees in water.

I rejoined Dick, he was fine and I communicated and found out that he was feeling good. When I had left for the surface, he had been fully conscious. He was now alert and had full realisation of what had happened and where and what he was doing. I started to pinch him to see what numbness he still had in his body. I could see that after some 10-15 minutes at 31 meters, his condition was no longer life threatening. That was a great relief as I know that had he died underwater then the world would probably blame me.

We spent the next few hours ascending slowly to the various stops on the planned table. All the time Dick was improving. We were suspended in mid water which was totally black, apart from our torch. I liken it to a light bulb being suspended in a pitch black mine shaft. The light attracted sea life like moths to a flame, including a couple of sharks. They came and went as did all the creatures and provided us something to look at. (Years later I joked with Dick that I wasn't worried about any predatory fish as I fancied my chances of out swimming him, especially as I tied him to the lazy shot!)

There was only one hiccup with the re-supply of cylinders. When we were approaching a change over point I could usually see the cylinders somewhere in the torch beam. On one occasion I couldn't see them anywhere. I indicated to Dick that I was going to the surface. When I reached the boat, the wind and sea were still raging. I shouted at Vic, "Where's the effing cylinders?" He said they were down there and showed me the rope on which they were suspended.

It then became clear what had happened. The hurricane winds had slowly pushed the boat onshore towards the reef, as soon as the depth became less than 50 meters, the anchor cable which we had used as a downline had become fixed to the bottom. The boat still got blown towards the shore, resulting in the downline now being at an angle. Anything now coming from the boat on a vertical line would get further from the downline the deeper it became. It was easily remedied and we continued without any further hiccups.

When we reached the shallower stops, the boats movements became jerked, we were no longer rolling with the sea gently but were fixed on the bottom. The huge height of the waves also made the stops inaccurate. Dick was feeling discomfort from the chafing of his lifeline. I therefore aborted the therapy, we had achieved 95% of our target and any further continual jerking on the lifeline would only have made things worse. We took him back onshore and observed him for 30 hours. His wife met us on the jetty where she had waited all night for him. He was out of immediate danger. During the period of observation his left arm was fully recovered, he had feeling back in his legs but was not strong enough to support his own weight.

He still had some numbness, spasms, prickles and some blurred vision. He was also very sore. I decided to take him back underwater to carry out a complete table 81, which was a full Therapeutic table in the BR 2806.

The crew left on the cay were telling me how severe the storm had been, like I had just returned from outer space, I told them not to be divas, I pointed out that it couldn't have been that bad as the beach Bar was still there and in true Caribbean fashion that was held together by string and sticky tape.

As we prepared for the new therapy another storm blew up, but at least it was daylight.

Table 81 was longer than the emergency table we had previously done but we had some 30 hours of detailed preparation and planning. The whole operation involved seven changes of cylinders each and was incident free. To my disappointment, Dick showed little signs of further recovery or improvement. On 9 August 1981, his company sent him down a Lear jet which flew him at low level back to his home in New Orleans.

Once there he was transferred to a brand new divers Alert Network (DAN) facility at the Jo Ellen Smith memorial Hospital. The facility was so new that Dick was their first hyperbaric patient.

An artist impression of the improvised "Lazy Shot" system which I used during the rescue of Dick Alba.

Dick and I standing outside the chamber at the DAN facility in New Orleans

On 17 February the following year, I was invited to the DAN facility as the Guest of Honour at the official opening. The doctors at the centre informed me that the action carried out in Belize had completely removed the nitrogen from dick Albas system, which had given him mobility, despite the residual damage to the spinal cord which had occurred before he reached me.

As you will have already read, I was sent to Belize as a punishment to get me out of the way. You will read what happened upon my return in the next but one chapter.

It is suffice to say that the last couple of dives I ever did as a British Army diver was the therapeutic treatments I had given to Dick Alba. Even though the Army Diving School wanted to discipline me for diving when the multi talented and experienced

Captain Bran (28 hours in his logbook!) ordered me not to, however I wouldn't have changed a thing.

Dick Alba.

I would like to add a little about Dick Alba. Subsequent to the rescue we became good friends and I sort of became an honorary member of his family.

Dick was a well renown and experienced commercial diver who ran his own diving company in New Orleans. Many may ask why such an experienced diver could get the bends but Dick had done his dives using a computer, which was then new to recreational diving, and it had shown that he was clear to ascend.

He was in the process of patenting his own invention of being able to take oil from a pipeline whilst it is still in use. The process is called "Hot Tapping" and at that time nobody had thought of a way to do it. It involved a method of trepanning with hydraulics.

He was also known for his ability as an underwater cutter/burner of pipelines. I was once asked what is the best method of removing piled oilrig legs 2 meters below the seabed. I thought about it and offered two methods which were both 'wrong' as they were too expensive. When I asked Dick the same question he spoke to me like the 'old man of the sea'. He said, "Aaaaah, that's the one job that separates the men from the boys." He went on to explain how it was done.

It entailed sending a diver down inside of the circular hollow leg with cutting gear, when he was at a depth which was 2 meters lower than the seabed he would cut a 360 degree circle, through the metal leg. The diver would return to the platform and watch as the crane would take up the slack and then hopefully bring up the leg. This would only happen if the cut was good add accurate, if the leg didn't come free then another diver, usually Dick, would have to go down and complete the job. He would have to cut below the previous attempt. This meant that when the leg eventually surfaced, all on the rig could see the failed attempt. Sometimes it was so bad that the diver was instantly sacked from his job. Commercial diving in these times was often a dog eat dog business.

In those early days of commercial diving in the gulf off New Orleans, many innovative and good practices were introduced. The area was going a decade or so before the North Sea and many of the practices were then used from the USA oil fields. The pioneer of the new diving helmets was a guy called 'Ratcliff e'. He devised his own commercial diving helmet which revolutionised oil diving. It was called the 'Rat Hat'. Dick owned a Rat Hat and kept it in pristine condition in his garage. I admired it and in a weak moment he gave it too me. It was a fantastic gesture but wrong Dick had a son, Richard Junior who is a fantastic guy. I had a quiet word, I said "listen mate, you have a son and that helmet is his and that's the end of it". He eventually agreed and it was the right thing.

Both Dick and his wife Marcie remained good friends. After my sacking from the Army when we were hopelessly poor and almost destitute, they gave us enormous support, Dick owed me nothing except his thanks and a handshake. He did however present me with a Rolex 'sea dweller' diving watch which I still wear proudly to this day. (It even takes priority over a gold Rolex given to me by HRH The Emir of Bahrain, but that's another story.)

We remained in close contact and on 3 November 1999 I received the news that Dick had become very ill and weak and had lapsed into a life threatening condition. I immediately booked a flight to New Orleans, and over the coming weekend I flew to see him. I was met at the airport by his youngest daughter who warned me that he was terribly emaciated. When I got to his house and entered his bedroom I could see instantly that she was right. He looked awful, like one of the people seen in the photos at the freeing of Belsen concentration camp. It was all made worse by the gloomy and unlit room he was lying in. I hugged and kissed him. I said "This is no bloody good in here, you can't see the sky, feel the wind or hear the birds," I then opened the shutters and window on to a beautiful Louisiana cloudless day. The room lit up the air was fresh and the place became alive. I had kind of taken over, not from arrogance, (heaven forbid) but I knew that nobody loved life more than Dick and I just wanted to put a little bit into that room. Nobody disagreed and many of them said that that was what was needed but that they were too close to the situation to do it.

I was only there for two days and it went very quickly. It had seemed like I had only just arrived and then I went in to say farewell. I sat on his bed and we both of course knew we would never see each other again. It was hard. Often in such sad and disturbing and stressful times and occasions I use humour to break the awfulness. I said to Dick, "I'll see you mate, take care and I really wanted the Rat Hat. !!!" Dick cried like a baby, I told him to stop being a handbag and to shove the helmet where the sun don't shine. I kissed him and told him I loved him for the last time and turned and walked away. I never looked back, tears streamed down my face en-route to the airport. I was back in my Army unit the next day. Dick died on 22 December 1999. He had lived for another 18+ years after coming to me by landing unconscious in the Puma helicopter as a stranger, during a stormy night on 3 August 1981.

Back to Marchwood.

I wrote an account of the rescue and sent it as an incident report to POM. I was governed by rules on incident reporting to do so. When I returned to Marchwood, I was sacked from Army diving and sent at five days notice to a unit at Dover. My diving pay was stopped, resulting in hardship for my family. Gary and Sarah had to change schools. We had just bought a house in Lincoln, which we struggled to keep but eventually had to sell. Captain Bran made it known that I should be disciplined for diving when he had forbidden me. As I was in the public eye, he was told to wind his neck in. One thing about the Army, for those who do not know, is that the officer corps, similar to the navy doctors, never openly contradicts or criticise each other. It was on this basis that I arrived in Dover.

Before I left Marchwood, Captain Bray gave me my annual report. It was quite awful. I told him that it was ridiculous. It stated things like 'lacked initiative', 'only average fitness' and 'below average' on a lot of topics. Not only was it part of the stitch up, it was insulting. When I asked why the report did not mention the rescue in Belize he said, 'We've only heard rumours'.

The annual report is called a confidential, and such a bad report would never allow anyone to recover their career. It was POM's way of poisoning the well for me and it was done out of spite. Captain Bray was a weak character. As soon as I started to prove that the report was clearly inaccurate by the stating facts, he put me in front of POM. This was definitely what they expected and I walked in to their trap, but I was furious at the injustice of the system that allowed them to get away with it. Five days later I was in Dover, having lost all the diving pay and after giving eighteen years of loyalty and energy to Army diving. I felt that it had all been for nothing.

It soon became apparent that POM had been busy on the telephone to the hierarchy at Dover and their minds were already made up. It was a terrible injustice, and even at Dover where I was training junior soldiers, POM had poisoned the well. From that moment on, even though I stayed in the Army for many more years, apart from one very noticeable exception, I was never ever able to trust an Army officer again.

New Orleans

Whilst I was at Dover, the news that I was British Diver of the Year was announced and I was awarded the Queen's Commendation for Brave Conduct. At the time of the announcement I was in New Orleans as a guest at the opening of the new DAN Hyperbaric medical facility, (mentioned earlier.) Dick and I were still closely in touch. He still had some residual damage from the injury, but at least he was still alive.

When the news that I was to receive the Queen's Commendation was published, it was on the front page of the Telegraph. Peter Barton, the head of British Airways in the United States contacted me. He congratulated me and asked if I would mind being upgraded to first class for the flight back. Of course I did not mind. He met me at the airport and took me in to the VIP lounge, which was a new experience for me. There were leather seats, a never ending buffet and every drink imaginable, and even some that were not. He gave me a collection of goodies and then introduced me to the pilot, a guy called Simon Sisnett. It was whispered to me that his family had some connection to Tate and Lyle Sugar in Jamaica. Quite frankly, I was awe-struck. It was like a dream. Later, I looked at my watch and said something quite daft. I looked at Peter Barton and said 'Hadn't we better make a move? It's getting on.' Simon Sisnett looked at me and said, 'I think we'll be all right. I'm flying the plane.' I felt a real idiot!

On board I was shown to a huge leather chair, like Jimmy Saville's on Jim'll Fix It. (Remember him?) The steward said

'Fancy a drink?' I did not know whether he meant water or tea! He said 'Bucks Fizz?' Then a stewardess came up and said 'Captain's compliments. Would you like to join them on the flight deck for take off?' I accepted and had a once in a lifetime experience of sitting in the cockpit for a night time take off over New Orleans. The meals, with a huge menu and silver cutlery, all added to the special ambience. It was a wonderful experience and I thank all those who made it possible. Just think, some people have that all their lives, but maybe if you do that all the time then nothing becomes special anymore.

I returned from New Orleans. Upon arriving back at Dover Annie told me that I was now quite a celebrity, and that the two local television companies wanted me to do a filmed interview.

Whilst I was away, a tabloid newspaper had wanted to interview me. I was not there but they spoke to Annie. Now the Army had a dilemma. I was suddenly flavour of the month and in demand, yet had ended up at Dover as a punishment posting, having been the victim of a huge injustice. They had a problem. What if I decided to tell the truth about the whole sordid affair on camera to the whole world? They could not risk it. They therefore arranged for Annie to be interviewed in the Officer Commanding's office. When the telephone rang he held her arm and said 'No grievances hinny,' (he was from the northeast). Every time I was interviewed, officer minders from an outside unit surrounded me. It was such a crude attempt to stop the truth coming out that an east European police state would have been proud.

The crude attempt at gagging me was disgusting and showed me that the Army knew that it was a disgrace and did not want it to get out to the public.

This proves that they knew it was a wrong, and none of them did anything about it.

Sadly this tale has a couple more turns. I knew that I could have spoken out about the injustice, had my say and had my day, but it was made clear that any such thing would be classed as disloyalty, and whatever career I had left would go up in flames. Also remembered that we as a family had just been shunted with five days notice. We had lost our house in Lincoln and, in an attempt to earn a few more pennies, I was working during leaves and holidays in Dover docks. Annie had gone fruit picking and had damaged her hernia and was waiting to go in to hospital for an operation. All of this was a result of the spiteful attack from POM and his acolytes. We could not take another move into some backwoods.

We were done.

One month later I collapsed at work. I do not know why or how. In every dustbin you can find a daffodil. When I came to, the camp doctor was tending me. He was a civilian and had had experience in the United States where he had a practice in California. He was the ringside doctor for several of the Muhammad Ali heavyweight fights. He was a very genuine man called Dr. Douglas Bilbey. He learned of my history with the diving fiasco.

At that time POM, as Superintendent of Diving, had even banned me from doing recreational diving. He could do this as long as I was in the Army. I wanted to continue to dive even without money, and sport diving would allow me to do this. At the time, Douglas Bilbey was carrying out all the diving medicals for the divers in the garrison of Dover, both military and sports diving. He gave me a diving medical and sent me to the head radiologist at a hospital in Dover without giving any history. The radiologist returned the x-rays 'passed fit to dive'. He then passed me my off shore diving medical. He also sent the x-rays, in confidence, to the top radiologist in the Army. He was a Major General stationed in Woolwich, whom he knew. It was returned as 'fit to dive'. How much more proof did I need that I had been stitched up? He sent the medical results to POM, and was told that the Diving School would only accept diving medicals by doctors who had done the Diving Medicine Doctors Course with the Navy at the Royal Navy Physiological Laboratories (RNPL). Douglas Bilbey attended the next course and came top. He then re-sent my passed medical certificate to POM. He returned it saying he would only accept the findings of a Royal Navy doctor. We then had a situation where the highly qualified Douglas Bilbey carried out all the diving medicals in Dover garrison including mine, and the diving school accepting all the findings except mine. It was not a great surprise but certainly proves beyond any doubt what a spiteful stitch up it was, by a moody tyrant and his unqualified acolytes.

At the time of my sacking I had twice as many recorded diving hours as any other army diver.

However, on a more positive front, the then head of Army sports diving, a guy called Peter Ormeroyd, visited Captain Bran and threw my medical results in front of him saying 'Look here! How much longer is this farce with Liddicoat going to continue?' He left that meeting and told me, 'You can now do sports diving.' It was fantastic news.

****

INTERIM STATEMENT BY: DOCTOR DOUGLAS BILBEY

It must be very unusual to interject in the writing of a book in this way: however I was reading the account in which Tony mentions me, Dr. Douglas Bilbey; and although accurate in all details, it does not exactly explain how I came onto the scene and quite an amount of drama which was forthcoming.

In 1980 I was appointed the Civilian Medical Officer to the Royal engineers, Junior Leaders Regiment at Dover. Up to that time I had an exotic and exciting medical career, having served as sub-dean of Medical Sciences at Kings College London; Professor of Anatomy at Toronto University, and holding a most successful general practice in Las Vegas, Nevada. It was the death of my wife Pearl from cancer that led to my application and acceptance of the job. It took me back to my beloved country, provided the social and physical enjoyments inherent in a military milieu and I was being mentally challenged.

Tony Liddicoat suddenly came on the scene as a young staff sergeant with aggressive and frustrating problems.

It was apparent, that in common parlance "he had been given a raw deal". The Army and Naval authorities had accepted certain recommendations from his then 'superior' and they were not going to retract their position.

I examined Tony and found him to be as fit as a fiddle. The X ray shadow, which was that of a hamartoma, was not present on most of his earlier X ray films as it was only apparent from a specific angle.

I made an official statement of my findings and was supported by a number of eminent radiologists from Shornecliffe and the Army medical headquarters at Woolwich. A rather nasty statement was forthcoming to the effect that 'the Naval medical decision could not be questioned' and that 'I as an unqualified physician in underwater medicine was to desist in the case'.

All this was too much of a challenge to my ego. I hated to lose and moreover I hated to see Tony and his family treated so unfairly.

So I applied and was given a submarine medical course at Portsmouth. It was a gruelling and at my age, fatiguing experience. The scientific and medical side was simple, however the physical effort was torture. I survived and took first place and became a certified 'under-water qualified physician'.

As such in the late 1980's I accompanied Tony's team of divers to Scapa Flow where they provided me with a daily feast of scallops.

To put all Tony's problems in a nutshell,' he had never had a medical problem diving either before or after the fortuitous discovery of a 'shadow' on his chest X ray.

****

Army Diving, the End

You will not believe what happened next.

I was busy at work with my troop when I got a message to report to the adjutant. The adjutant sits in an office next to the commanding officer and, for want of a better adjective, is his lackie.

I went into his office and he said that the Army Display was on at Aldershot and that I was required to go and front the display diving tank, answer questions and sing the praises of army diving to the crowds of visitors.

I looked at him as if he was some sort of idiot. I explained that surely he had got the wrong man and it must be a wind-up. He looked away and said 'Be there at ten o'clock tomorrow Staff . It's a direct order' (A direct order is a last ditch tool used by the untalented in the military to get something done, which is sometimes illegal, and most of the time plain ridiculous). To disobey generally resulted in severe punishment. I could therefore do nothing but attend or else. The next day I set of early to make it look as if I intended to be at the show by ten o'clock. If POM the tyrant had any thoughts that the direct order would make me compliant then, as the annual report he wrote proved, he did not know me at all. I got to Camberley, near Aldershot, and called in to see my sister and have a cup of tea. I gathered my thoughts and telephoned the guardroom at Dover. I explained who I was and that whilst en route to the Army show my car had broken down and I was unable to fix it. I had no idea how long I was going to be stuck, so they should immediately telephone the adjutant and explain the situation. I drank my cup of tea and returned home to Dover.

I heard nothing more about it.

I never bothered to regain any position in Army diving. After eighteen years it was the end. The five-day move with my family cost us dear in health and stress and, to this day, I cannot forgive the individuals concerned or the system that can allow such things to happen.

I also learned that loyalty in the army was a much-vaunted single-edged sword. You are expected to give it unconditionally but you should not expect it in return. What was frustrating beyond belief for me was the impotence of my position. I was totally unable to do anything. I have witnessed hundreds of injustices in the Army towards its own soldiers. They have no system of redress open to them. The system screams for an independent ombudsman, but that would make the POMs of this world accountable, which is the last thing they would want. It was not until many years later, whilst attending my daughters' degree investiture, that I watched a group of new doctors (including a few in naval uniform) recite an oath out loud. I later discovered it was called the Hippocratic Oath and they all faithfully promised and swore by this oath. If I had known about this at the time, I would have produced laminated copies and distributed them to certain surgeon commanders in the navy who treated me, just to tell them that I may be a nobody and a lower rank to them, but I am still somebody to my family. I would then have asked why they chose to ignore the oath to which they had sworn. None of those I met had the moral courage to contradict another Naval doctor, yet beyond their ivory tower all the specialists I saw, without exception, told me that I was fit to dive and explained why. Something should be done about such blind adherence to their freemason type allegiance to each other.

It ended a sad and disgraceful episode within the British military system.

I have been advised by people whose opinion I value to move on with the book once the chapter has been written. However, the episode had to be included.

The fact that it was done deliberately sticks in the craw, and I liken it to an assassination attempt that will always be with me.

I shall now move on with the book, as I did with my life.

I am presented with "Diver of the Year" by the BSAC's Mike Todd, whilst stationed at Dover.

As a result of a request of the press I pose in diving kit at the Dover wimming pool where I first started diving all those years ago. Looking on Annie, Sarah and Paula.

1982-2000

Folkestone, a New Beginning

I was in Dover. It was a Wednesday and I was sitting at home. I thought I would try to join a local subaqua club. I looked up the clubs in Dover and Folkestone. Dover met on a Tuesday and Folkestone met on a Wednesday. It was Wednesday, so Folkestone it was. I looked up the address and bought a street map of Folkestone to find the route, and that evening I drove into the town.

It was a decision made partly by luck and partly by coincidence that I ended up at Folkestone. However, it turned out to be one of the best decisions I ever made. It was 1982 and even now in 2006, almost twenty-five years later, I am off to the Red Sea in a couple of months to dive with a group from Folkestone. Such is my fervour and friendship for the club and its members, but I do have to admit now that it was a huge culture shock for me at the time.

Coming from a background of strict discipline, punctuality and fitness as I had, to mixing with this multicultural group of irreverent Herberts was an experience and a culture shock. However, they proved to be, in their own way, very adept, professional and talented. They brought a wide cross-section of skills and enthusiasm to the club. The diving was done in a radius from Folkestone. The clubhouse was shared between the Folkestone Yacht and Motor Boat Club (FYMBC) and BSAC 501. They had their own hard boat in those days which, years later, they updated by buying a much larger hulled vessel. They fitted it out themselves to make it a much grander, superb diving boat. Folkestone is tidal and has an inner harbour that dries out at low tides, so all the diving is tidal and requires good chart reading and excellent seamanship and boat handling.

Waiting for the tide to come in and lift the boat off the mud of the inner harbour Folkestone' 0500 on a Saturday morning.

Some of the team pose on the stern en-route to the dive site.

These were the days before RHIBS, sonar and satellite navigation, and we would chug out in 501 Diver (the boat's name) and take bearings from land transits to position ourselves on one of the many wrecks. Sometimes in the early morning the coastal mist had not burned off by the time of the dive and we could not see the land transits. We would have to go back inshore to dive on a wreck easily found, closer to the shore.

One such wreck was the Orangeman. It had sunk with a cargo of oranges that washed up on the beach for weeks, hence its name.

I was starting to become fascinated with wrecks and their histories. I wanted to know more about them and started to keep papers on them, and then files. It became a sort of obsession. When you dive on a wreck you find a time capsule recording the very moment it sank. Even though there would have been a collapse of the superstructure and corrosion over the years, you could still build up an accurate picture of what life was like and get an idea of how the ship was built.

In many cases, the records of the wreck's name and location of sinking were quite inaccurate. A couple of good examples were the Titanic and the Bismarck. These two famous wrecks took many years to find, even though there were hundreds of witnesses to the sinkings. Accurately naming some of the many wrecks around Folkstone was still difficult. We would look at the artefacts brought up and try to identify the silhouette of the superstructure. The only sure place to find the name of a ship was the bell. All bells have the launch name of the ship on them, so if you find the bell you have the launch name.

However, a ship may have changed hands several times and have been renamed each time. Usually, the new name would be painted on, but rarely was the bell changed. Therefore, whilst the launch name gives you a clue, that is all it is. Sometimes there were many ships with the same name, particularly if that name was popular at the time.

When we were not diving, we were researching and sourcing data and information. In those days there was no internet, so the main sources for reference were local libraries, newspaper archives and Lloyds of London. When locating wrecks, the local fisherman proved an invaluable source of information. They knew most of the wreck sites, having fished them for years. If a good rapport exists between the two communities of divers and fishermen, there is a lot to be achieved by mutual scratching. However, the most dangerous job ever attempted by amateur sports divers is the recovery of fishing nets from obstructions under water and requests to do this are very common.

The early times at Folkestone opened up a whole new diving world for me and it became very addictive. I was then posted from Dover to Chatham in Kent, so was still able to commute down to Folkestone and continue diving. I recovered my first porthole, a momentous occasion for any diver. Like all first portholes, I feverishly polished it until it was like glass. Many dives were on a Lightship LV 75, which used to mark the access to

Folkestone. In those days it was a popular dive because it was quite close inshore and could be dived at any time, due to the easily seen land transits. The vessel had been sunk by a German bomber during the last world war.

This is a true story from the LV 75. During one particular dive, a diver called Bob rested his hand on a piece of wreckage. On closer examination it was found to be the ship's bell, not easily identifiable as it was covered in crustaceans and molluscs. The next dive Bob descended with a hacksaw and sawed through the two brackets holding the bell in place. When he got the bell home and started to clean it up he found that the two brackets he had sawn through were ornate dolphins, which framed the bell and held it by their tails. The next dive he went down with an adjustable spanner and unbolted the brackets and brazed them back on. This is a simple example to show how items are not recognisable when viewed from an unusual angle (The vessel was on its side) The diving continued with everyone attending as often as they could. Often we would be sitting on the boat, which was beached on the mud or sand of the inner harbour, waiting and watching for the tide to come in and lift us off . We very often met at dawn and finished at dusk. They were halcyon days of wreck diving and, apart from great diving, the craic and humour were great. Many of the stories and anecdotes from those times still make me laugh today.

A great character worthy of mention was the club diving officer, Nigel Wilkins. Even now, as I write this book with some forty-five years of diving experience, I have never met anyone who was a better diving officer than Nigel. He still dives with the club, as does his son Mark, and even though he is now in his seventies, he is still in good shape and an excellent diver.

I was stationed at Chatham in the Field Engineering wing as an instructor and had been promoted to Warrant Officer Class Two. Initially, I was instructing on bridging, whilst also running a course for Senior Staff Sergeants who were waiting to become Warrant Officers. The Watermanship Training Centre was at another branch of the school. This was responsible for teaching Army students basic and advanced watermanship, boat operating and handling, and craft operating. A Warrant Officer (WO) vacancy to be in charge of the centre came and I was given the job. I must admit that, with an eighteen-year history of handling diving boats, it was a subject that was close to my heart and I was delighted with the appointment. The first thing I did was to attend our own course, the Craft Operators Course 84/1 at the centre. It was a testing course, with both theory and practical tests, and I realised that I had a good team of instructors.

The main work craft of the Army at that time was called the Combat Support Boat (CSB), which was an extremely fast and manoeuvrable craft. We covered all the main watermanship topics: navigation, chart reading, boat handling, etc, and the course included a navigation exercise to the Essex coast, Southend and Canvey Island. It was a fun day and skimming about on the river and sea in the Combat Support Boat was very exhilarating. To gain experience in open sea and a tidal rip, as well as strong currents, the course spent a week at Weymouth, my old stomping ground from where I used to run the Army diving courses. The week at Weymouth was always fun and I used to load up my diving kit and dive from a Combat Support Boat around Portland Bill and on the Lulworth Banks to collect scallops. I would then bring them back, cook them and share them with the team. Scallops remain my favourite seafood, a taste dating from my earlier days in Scotland.

I came to know Weymouth well, from the helicopter recovery in 1974 to running the diving courses in 1980, and knew where to find good safe diving.

One weekend I took a dive charter boat out to the wreck of the Salsette and dived with Hampstead BSAC. It was easy to understand why people flocked down to the wide part of the channel to dive as opposed to the narrows of the straits of Dover. There was hardly any current and the visibility was about eight metres. The Salsette was an old P&O passenger liner and still looked magnificent in all its splendour at forty-four metres.

The wrecks off Folkestone were abundant and historic, and too many to mention, but we had our favourites. The Pommerania was a first class mail steamer, the Anglia a hospital ship, the Northfleet was carrying immigrants to Australia, the Grosser Kurfurst was the German fleet's flagship, the Seine was full of champagne. The list is endless.

The champagne wreck attracted much attention, here I am with my son Gary in a photo taken for an article in the British Army magazine 'Soldier'

Here I am on the cover of the British Army magazine 'Soldier', seemingly trying to approve the advantages of mixing diving and alcohol.

However, one wreck dive that will always live in my memory was on Saturday the second of July 1983. We set off in 501 Diver. The channel was flat calm, like a mirror. We reached the dive site and threw in a shot and buoy to mark where the wreck should be. We then circled the buoy until we picked up the wreckage on the echo sounder. Once we were directly over the wreck site, we threw in the wreck anchor, pulled it taut proving that it had snagged the wreck and moved the boat to it. We then dived using the anchor line as a down line, which the divers would use to descend to and ascend from the wreck. The club members at 501 were very proficient and expert in all aspects of wreck diving and I learned much from them.

On this occasion I happened to be one of the first pairs down the line. The underwater visibility for the area was fantastic, some six to eight metres. The ship was sitting upright and looked undamaged. It was a three-islander silhouette, and whilst swimming along the open gangways of the centre island I picked up two intact portholes. This was a success as many of the wrecks had been sunk as a result of being bombed, mined or torpedoed during wars. All of these cause huge explosions, which usually shatter the glass in the portholes. Therefore, finding two intact portholes so easily was very pleasing.

When I swam into the bridge I found the ship's sextant and popped it into my goody bag. It was an excellent find. It was a great dive and everyone found something special. The water was still flat clam as we chugged our way back to Folkestone. We all decided to dive it again after the six-hour surface interval, so we had to return to charge the air cylinders.

A humorous side of this second dive decision was that those who had planned things on the domestic front had to phone their excuses to whoever was waiting for them. There was a queue at the clubhouse payphone. Peter, a schoolteacher, was one of the divers going for the second dive. He had only spoken about five words when the line went dead as his wife slammed the phone down. He did not live far away, so I asked him if he was going to pop home and explain. He replied 'No, I think visual contact may be more than she can handle.' I told you this wreck diving lark was addictive! We dived again in the evening, and I found a phosphor bronze ship's wheel and stand. We discovered that the name of the ship was the Nunima, and it had sunk after a collision in fog.

Schoolteacher Peter found the much sought after bell. This was no coincidence, as I believe that he has found and owns some four ship's bells to date. (Nunima was written on the bell found that day). Even though he is a friendly and affable guy, and an excellent diver, all the other divers in the club who do not own a bell really quite dislike him!

Army Sport Diving Expeditions: Bovisand and Scapa Flow

I was still able to dive within the army as a sports diver. I enjoyed it and could do it with absolute peace of mind from a medical point of view.

Five independent diving medical doctors had passed me fit to dive. Their reassurance had lifted a huge weight from my mind. It is not that I had only wanted the doctors to say what I wanted to hear. If any of the doctors, radiologists or specialists had said to me, 'Listen, for your own good stop diving,' I would have stopped, but the evidence proving me fit to dive was so overwhelming that I continued to do so safely and wholeheartedly. The statement 'I would not recommend this man for submarine escape training' remains the only negative comment I ever had.

Nevertheless, I was a married man with a family and was in no position to take unnecessary risks and would never have done so. I was therefore permitted to do sports diving activities whilst on duty, which was a legal necessity whilst I was still in the Army.

Due to the official clearance gained for me by Peter Ormeroyd, I could still attend and participate in diving expeditions. I was still an active Sub Aqua Diving Supervisor (SADS), and Army sports diving rules required that a Sub Aqua Diving Supervisor be in attendance whenever sports diving took place. An army unit based at Folkestone was planning a sports diving expedition to Bovisand, Plymouth, where there was an ideal centre, with accommodation and equipment, administered by the Joint Services Diving Centre. I went down there to act as Sub Aqua Diving Supervisor and we had a successful expedition, training up novices to achieve the Sport Diver qualification.

In May 1984 I travelled to Scapa Flow and spent a couple of days diving on two very old wrecks in what used to be the main anchorage for the British Atlantic Fleet during the last century.

At the end of the First World War, the entire German High Seas Fleet was interned in the Flow and scuttled itself. It was the largest ever single loss of shipping in one act, fifty two ships in total. Many of the wrecks had been heroically salvaged between the wars, but there were still some German dreadnoughts there.

Additionally, the wrecks of the British warships, Royal Oak (sunk by a German submarine) and HMS Vanguard (sunk as the result of an internal explosion) are located there. Therefore, there was a lot of history, great wrecks and fantastic diving opportunities in relatively good visibility, with little if any current. It had been on my 'to do' list ever since I read about it, and I initially went there for a couple of days to sound out accommodation and boat hire.

I found a small military camp with wooden huts called Ness Battery, (Years later Ness Battery camp was sold by the military, I tried very hard to buy it and even put in the highest bid, but as these things often turn out, it was a done deal and the council had got it even though their bid was lower than mine.) which was tailor-made for self-contained expeditions. I then planned and organised an expedition; intent on taking with us everything we needed to be self reliant. We would take our own cook, mechanic, doctor, diving kit, vehicles and drivers. We would be accommodated in the Officers Mess hut, which had its own coal-fired central heating. The military had an on site warden and keeper for the property, a Mr Linklater who lived in the nearby town of Stromness. I recruited from my local regiment in Chatham where I was based, and we assembled a good team. A road party drove up, and the rest of us went up by rail on the overnight sleeper. We then caught the local car ferry from Thurso to Stromness, which sailed up alongside the island of Hoy with its magnificent cliff s and the craggy monument The Old Man of Hoy.

We moved into the camp and everything was there waiting for us. We had spent weeks collecting and scrounging what we could. My Sergeants Mess had donated a barrel of beer for the bar and many Army cookhouses had given us spare rations. We were given a freezer full of meat (the guy in charge of the Bovisand expedition was a catering officer, so mutual scratching was prominent). We took up spare parts of all kinds, which would save us from having to spend our own pennies. I took up Annie and the kids, and we had our own suite. I invited members from the Folkestone club and many of them came along. The doctor was Douglas Bilbey, who I had met at Dover on my last posting, and had become a firm friend. It was an assembly of a great bunch. We had been given the use of a trawler called the Crombie at a much reduced hire rate on the proviso that we give it a spring clean.

Nigel Wilkins and his wife Joy attended. Joy was a non-diver but used her excellent photographic skills to become the expedition photographer. We would be required to produce media articles and a report at the end of the expedition. The diving was excellent and we managed to dive all the remaining German ships in their huge silent glory.

The diving Liddicoats at Scapa Flow.

Additionally, there was plenty of other good diving on the blockade ships (sunk to deny access to the sound by enemy ships) and several of the little beaches and coves. Après diving was also excellent. We visited a Viking settlement at Skara Brae, the Italian Chapel on the Churchill Barriers and the Tomb of the Eagles on the most southerly tip of the islands.

We were there for two weeks. On the middle Sunday I proposed laying a wreath at the memorial in Kirkwall Cathedral to the eight hundred and thirty three men who lost their lives during the Royal Oak disaster during the Second World War. The wreck is now an official war grave, but the bell has been recovered and is the centrepiece of the memorial in the cathedral. I thought it only right, as a service expedition, that we should go and pay our respects. We donned our Sunday best and drove over there, only to find the place was closed. We eventually found the Bishop and explained what we would like to do. He opened the cathedral up and we were able to pay our respects. We had clubbed together and bought an anchor-shaped wreath. I remarked to the Bishop that I was surprised to find him closed on a Sunday. He said 'Well you have to have one day off .' I thought that, being a house of worship, Sunday would be its big day, and perhaps it would be better to close on a Monday. It was like a pub closing on a Saturday night! I thought it, but did not say anything because I did not want to offend.

The Orkneys have a lot to offer. Ness Battery Camp was used during the last war to house Italian prisoners of war. They were tasked to build a system of causeways between the islands to make them totally impenetrable by enemy craft. The previously used blockade ships were a deterrent but they did not stop Gunther Prien and his German submarine from sneaking in and firing the torpedoes that sank the Royal Oak. The Italian prisoners had decorated the dining hall at Ness Battery Camp with alpine scenes from their native Italy. They also converted a nissen hut in to a chapel that can still be visited today.

Outside the Flow is the wreck of HMS Hampshire, which sank after a mystery explosion on board. There was terrible loss of life, which included Lord Kitchener (Your Country Needs You). But the wreck lies too deep for any expedition with novices on it to dive and is dependant on having a calm sea.

The trawler, Crombie, was our base and, although a likeable old friend, it was in need of some tender loving care. The bridge windows were the vertical sliding and rising type, controlled by a leather strap (like old railway carriages). Some of the straps had broken and some of the external hinges on the seat lockers had rusted through and needed replacing. Therefore, for a very reasonable hire price, we agreed to refurbish what we could. In between dives we busied ourselves with those little jobs. It made quite a difference to the old tub.

Gary M was the expedition mechanic and he loved to be in the engine room, a black hole in the deck with a wooden ladder. At the start of the expedition he went into the engine compartment and removed three black sacks full of rubbish from a space no bigger than a prison cell. It was as if Rab C Nesbitt had squatted down there. We were able to make a big difference and it was a super dive platform, which also gave us a warm area to sit and a cooker to make hot drinks. I thought I became quite a good captain of the boat, but I regretted not being asked to perform any marriages or burials at sea! That apart, I enjoyed a lovely experience on the Crombie.

One of the dive boat operators had found a ship's stamp from one of the German Fleet wrecks, and it was good to be able to endorse our logbooks with it at the end of the expedition.

Being in Scotland, we had our fair share of scallops and fresh mushrooms from the fields around Ness Battery. It was a great expedition and even rewriting this now and reading through my logbooks brings back fond memories.

Around this time I was told a true story about the mismanagement and crooked dealings at the Army Diving School. POM had obviously meted out a diabolical decision to somebody, who had decided to write anonymously to the press. There was a huge effort to prevent this, and I was one of those interviewed by the Services Investigation Bureau (SIB). I had long left the school but I believe that they interviewed everyone. The investigation uncovered a whole trail of illegal and corrupt activities. Several officers, including my friend Captain Bran, had been granted diving pay without taking any of the courses. This was the standard preferential treatment for POM's favourites, and it exposed a whole hornet's nest of irregularities and shoddy treatment towards many people. It was just like hearing about a rogue dictator in a banana republic.

A former colleague told me that POM and Captain Bran had had a big disagreement that had become quite nasty (he was standing outside the door at the time). At least the abuse of power, like that which I had received, had been exposed.

Some time later I watched with horror as POM projected himself on a live television broadcast as the head of the Mary Rose recovery. The cradle lifting the wreck had collapsed due to a missing support pin and almost crushed the timber structure. Thankfully it was recovered, and is now on display in Portsmouth. However, it was achieved more by luck than precision diving, and it was obviously not checked prior to the lift.

POM made a joke about Tudor firewood, but it was far from being a well-executed operation, and the Mary Rose Trust divers I knew were quite angry and upset. What goes around comes around.

Falkland Islands

Army life continued and I was posted back to Germany as a Sergeant Major. The posting was brought forward by eight months because the unit I was joining was due to go to the Falkland Islands for a six month tour. Sadly, my stay at the Watermanship Training Centre was cut short, as I had really enjoyed the job. I went to Germany, whilst Annie and the family stayed in Chatham. The upheaval another move would cause did not make sense if they were to be left on their own when I went to the Falklands for the six to seven month tour. So off I went to Germany, alone.

One month later I was on my way to the Falklands. An aircraft to Ascension Island, refuelling at Dakar and then a ten day trip south in a troop ship. Whilst this book is primarily about diving, you may notice that I hardly ever mention anything about my parallel Army life. I highlighted the farcical injustice at the diving school, but the rest of my life in the Army has been glossed over.

I think that much can be said about the Army system and I will do that by writing a book specifically about the Army (currently planned to be called The Army Game, so keep a look out!).

The Falklands of 1984 to 1985, which was only just after the conflict, was an unbalanced place to be, and could bring out the worst in human nature. I took my diving kit and it proved to be a very good move in helping to keep me sane. The internet and mobile phones did not exist yet, and telephone links to the United Kingdom were unavailable, so the feeling of isolation was overpowering. It was a sad place, where the only outlet provided for the troops was alcohol. The diving, however, was quite breathtaking, and it is one of the best places in the world for clarity of water, variety of sealife and wrecks.

My unit controlled the diving team and the Combat Support Boats, so it was easy for me to go out and dive.

My first dive was in Sparrow Cove where Brunel's ship, SS Great Britain, had been dumped after her usefulness had ended. She was no longer there, having been towed away to be renovated and rebuilt. My Officer Commanding and Second in Command had said that they would like to try diving, and Sparrow Cove proved to be ideal for the purpose.

It was always my custom to take a small Army stove with me to cook whatever I had found on the shore or in the water. On the menu on that day were mussels, big tasty mussels.

I collected and boiled them in a tin can. There was no need to purge them, as you have to do with european mussels, because they were already clean. They tasted lovely, even though I had forgotten to bring an onion and a lemon along.

A strange fact with these mussels, which I have never found anywhere else, was that many of them contained tiny pearls. I kept some in an old film canister in case they ever became valuable (but I cannot find them now!). I have eaten mussels on the shores of nearly every ocean and sea in the world, and I have never come across the pearls again.

Outside the inner harbour and on the way to the South Atlantic Ocean is a rocky outcrop called Kelly's Rock. It was named after a ship called the John R Kelly, which struck the rock and sank. It became my main diving site for the next few months.

Near the outcrop was a large forest of kelp rising from the bottom on their huge single stalks and, nearer the top, the large broad leaves would grow and lie on the surface of the water, forming a roof on which oystercatcher birds walked. The Combat Support Boat used a jet propulsion system, which sucked in water and jetted it out for propulsion, so I had to anchor away from the kelp and travel to the wreck site and Kelly's Rock under water. It was like walking through a forest, gliding between the thick kelp stalks. On very sunny days when the sea was calm, the beams of sunlight would cascade down between the gaps in the leaves on the surface, reminiscent of a huge church or cathedral. The kelp was yellow-brown but glowed bright yellow in the sunlight.

The colours of the rocks varied from reds and purples to greens. Large chunks of timber from the wreckage had also been coloured like the rocks. It was difficult to orientate yourself around the wreck because the wreckage was broken and had spread. Whilst I found some porcelain door or drawer handles, a small brown glass phial for medicine, many trennells (wooden nails, derived from 'tree nails') and small bits and pieces, I never came across an identifiable part of the ship's structure. Nevertheless, the wreck was fascinating. Nowadays, the Falklands maritime museum sells porcelain inkwells recovered from the wreck, which sank in 1899.

On a couple of the dives I was joined by a seal, which had claimed Kelly's Rock as its own. It seemed friendly enough and looked just like a furry torpedo. The shells and sealife were new to me.

I remember coming across a large pyramid of small yellow shells. It looked as if someone had ladled a large pile of sweet corn onto the ocean floor. All of the shells were empty, and when a pair were laid on a flat surface, they resembled a small butterfly. During my time there I saw small red prawn-like creatures all over the kelp leaves and being eaten by seabirds that walked on the leaves. This was my first experience of Krill.

As has been well recorded, the winter in the South Atlantic produces some ferocious storms, to which I attributed the damage and spread of the wreckage. However, it did not uproot or seem to damage the kelp stalks, proving just how tough and strong they were. Even though I was there during summer, there was always a strong wind blowing and a choppy sea.

Being a qualified boat operator from my last job and having the ability to dive were two factors that made the Falklands tour bearable for me.

Diving training in the Falklands. A dive group returns to Port Stanley after carrying out aptitude dives in Sparrow Cove

The Falkland Islands is a graveyard for many wrecks which called into Port Stanley to lick their wounds after sailing around the southern route of South America

My final dive in the Falklands was really very memorable. I went out in a Combat Support Boat and anchored in the usual place. I heard a plopping sound and saw several dorsal fins from a school of dolphins. I dropped a shot line and, with my heart pounding at not knowing what to expect, I slid into the water as quietly as I possibly could so that I did not run the risk of provoking or frightening them, and descended. It was amazing. The school of piebald dolphins swam in a circle around me. (I took some slides of then as they circled me, but the results were hopeless, not my fault the dolphins wouldn't stay still, even though they were told,) The slides just show dark shadows which you need to hold up to a welding arc light to view! They were obviously curious and I must have looked a mystery to them. One female swam around me with her baby, as if to show it what to see. They circled for several minutes and left. It was a magical moment for me. (I now discover that the dolphins were called 'Commersons Dolphins'.)

For part of the tour in the Falklands, I had my Nikonos III underwater camera with me and tried to record what I saw, but whilst I am quite pleased with the results, I think they should stay secret!

Harz Mountains, Sardinia and Lake Titicaca

After the Falklands, it was back to Germany. My family joined me in the picturesque town of Iserlohn where my unit was stationed.

The appointment of Sergeant Major requires a great deal of commitment to people. They are important and will not wait in an in or out tray. For this reason my diving became a pursuit in free time only. I teamed up again with Olly, my German friend and dive buddy, who was still working as the equipment editor for the German diving magazine Taucher. Since we had last met I had gained some infamy as British Diver of the Year and had become involved with the Folkestone Sub Aqua Club. Olly was a good contact and we enjoyed a two day visit to Holland Diving in Amsterdam, which had its diving shop and swimming tank in an old church.

The Dutch diving magazine interviewed me and they wrote an article about the Caribbean rescue. I carried out some underwater welding in Holland and tried out their equipment. We did more dives in the Buddenkuhle and travelled up to Kiel. These were all well-known old haunts from my past.

Towards the end of my tour as Sergeant Major, I was selected for promotion to Warrant Officer Class One.

At the time there was no appointment vacant for me, so I had three months of marking time whilst I waited to join my new unit.

In the interim I returned to the Royal School of Military Engineering as an instructor. Recruiting was underway to take part in a sub aqua expedition to dive Lake Titicaca in South America. I asked my new boss for permission to apply for the expedition, which he granted. I thought that, as I was to spend some months in limbo awaiting my next job, there would be an opportunity to attend a big expedition. I sent in my application and was invited to attend a selection weekend in the Harz Mountains. The area was chosen because of its similarity to Lake Titicaca. The lakes in the Harz region were all at altitude, which requires slightly amended dive and decompression times.

I met up with an old friend from my days as an instructor at the Kiel diving unit, Roger Gill. Roger was a non-diver in the early days, but took to it in his later years and had done very well. He was also a very funny and quick-witted guy. The Harz was similar to the Lake District, very beautiful and a tourist attraction. We went to dive in a manmade lake where a dam had been constructed, forming a reservoir. The rising waters had engulfed a deserted village called Schulenberg, whose abandoned buildings and infrastructure were still there.

To gain access to the water's edge, we had to abseil down a steep slippery path with our diving kit. Roger was just above me on the rope and he uttered, 'I must put this dive in my climbing logbook.' The dive was awful. The water was ink black and the visibility was less than zero. As I have mentioned earlier, all mountain lakes are silt traps and are therefore usually not good diving. We carried out a couple of dives there, and I bought a coloured postcard of the village prior to being flooded to show what we could have seen.

I was selected as the Diving Officer for the main expedition to Titicaca.

The next stage was a meeting of those people who had been selected to attend a mini-expedition to Sardinia.

The leader of the expedition explained that we had been asked to test a new dive computer called Aladdin, which was made in Switzerland by a company called Uwatec. The Swiss are considered to be amongst the leaders in altitude diving in the world because most of their diving is done at altitude. The leader at producing tables for altitude was Dr Carl Buhlmann, who had pioneered the Buhlmann Dive Tables. They were to be used in the Aladdin computers. The Expedition's leader and I travelled to Switzerland and met both Dr Buhlmann and Uwatec. It was an interesting experience and we were well hosted by both parties. Until this time, 1986 to 1987, I had a somewhat jaundiced view of dive computers. The guy whom I rescued in the Caribbean had got into difficulty because he had relied upon an early version of a dive computer and he had ended up with a severe spinal bend due to trusting it. This was one of the reasons for my mistrust.

However, I could not fail to be impressed with the set up at Uwatec and the capabilities of the computer. The expedition was to be given one each to test, and we had to formally produce the test results for Uwatec.

The next stage was to assemble as a team on the southern most tip of Sardinia, in a tented camp for a two-week diving expedition.

The Army used to use Sardinia as an adventure training base and kept a pool of equipment at a Royal Air Force base called Decimomannou. We were to use that equipment to set up a camp on the beach.

You may think that a tented camp in Sardinia during spring would be an absolute breeze, with warm sunny days and T-shirt weather. Wrong! It has to go down as the coldest camping experience I have ever had. There was a constant biting wind and the temperature was well below freezing. A bowl of water that I had kept in our tent (shared with Roger Gill) overnight became a block of ice by the morning. A couple of the guys had not brought sleeping bags and had hurriedly borrowed thin tropical sleeping bags from the Royal Air Force base in Germany. The sleeping bags they borrowed were very light and had a look and feel to them like an oven glove. I slept in my huggy bear fleece undersuit as well as my own sleeping bag, and I still woke up at two or three o'clock shivering. I do not know whether it was just a freak cold snap or it is the same every year, but it was certainly bitterly cold.

I produced a dive programme and we began our training. On the first dive my own direct feed hose blew off and I had to carry out an emergency ascent. Thankfully, the hose was found on the next dive and I managed to repair it in a local car garage. There was no chance of using a dive shop or any sort of sophisticated hardware store. Everywhere was closed and hibernating until the summer. Tumbleweed even rolled through the streets, so desolate was the village. A non-diving doctor had been recruited, and one of the lads took him to the local bay to introduce him to diving. I left to take the others on a dive to a sunken statue of the Virgin Mary holding the infant Jesus. Local fishermen had placed it there to keep them safe and bring them luck. You may be imagining an Italian statue of the Madonna and Child carved in white marble rather like Michaelangelo's David, but you would be wrong.

It was made very crudely from cement and was quite a fright. We were using inflatable boats with plywood floors, which were called floppies They were fine to dive from and could be collapsed down into a valise, so were ideal for travelling to isolated places. The engine was placed on a stern transom, and connected to a fuel can by a fuel line with a bulbous squeeze feed.

The success of diving revolves around the mechanical reliability of both air compressors and boat engines. Boat engines have a habit of cutting out or stopping at the most inopportune moments. During this venture, six divers were fully kitted up in diving equipment and ready to get into the water in a floppy when the engine cut out. We were carried on to rocks by the swell and onshore wind. We started to fend off the rocks by using paddles, whilst the boat operator was desperately tugging on the starter rope to get the engine started again. In the process he caught Roger's eye with his elbow, resulting in a shiner. Things were not going well. Eventually we restarted the engine and completed the dive. The water clarity and sea life were super.

    When the dive was over we returned to the camp, passing a bay where the expedition doctor was being taken on a try dive. When I had seen them en route to the main dive, they had dropped a weight belt into the sand whilst trying to dress the doctor. The doctor and his instructor were standing side by side in waist deep water looking for the lost belt. When we came past the site again hours later, after the main dive, they were both standing at the same place, still looking for the belt. You could have sold tickets to watch that.

    There were danger signs to me, as the expedition diving officer, that several things were not right. The lads who had not been told to bring sleeping bags were suffering from the bitter cold. They were waking up in the early hours and sitting in the Landrover with the engine on and the heating turned up to try and keep warm. This woke up everyone else. We would build a campfire each evening and sit round it for warmth. One of the lads took a large boulder from the fire to take to bed for warmth. This was an old survival trick. However, you usually wrap the boulder in a towel to prevent it burning your skin.

This lad was so exhausted that he fell asleep with the unlagged rock and burnt his stomach. He had a burn blister the size of a dinner plate and was very uncomfortable. Some initiative was needed, like direct action, to get some suitable sleeping bags and warmer clothing, but nothing happened. The Expedition Leader had acquired a new type of padded coverall for all of us to wear. He boasted that it was made using space-age technology and would keep us all warm, and he had his with him. I asked where ours were and he said that he did not bring them because he wanted to keep them new. I asked 'Why bring only yours?' 'To test it', I was told.

It was a very selfish act not to give priority to the lads in the team who, because they were misinformed, were suffering from hypothermia and sleep depravation. It was a nonsense and alarm bells began to ring. I was worried in case we encountered problems that we had not addressed in Europe once we were isolated in South America. On the other side of the world where there are no easy answers and very little civilisation, we could end up with serious problems. The computers had arrived but the expedition leader kept them all in his tent, which was a double tent that we had all put up for him and he occupied alone. He kept all of the donations from the sponsors to himself.

Back to the diving. Situated perhaps a mile off shore was a large rock that was only just poking above the water. It had a lighthouse to warn boats of its existence but I could see that, over the centuries, many boats had foundered on it. It was a perfect shipping hazard, particularly at night. I planned to take the divers out there and have a good truffle hunt around its base for evidence of ancient shipwrecks. It was good diving and there was a lot of evidence of shipwrecks. Shards of amphorae, (old Mediterranean pottery) littered the seabed and were wedged in crevices. Every piece could have told a story.

We carried out a night dive. The Expedition Leader asked to dive with me. I was using my trusty old Avon dry suit with a zip entry, which was much easier and more practical than the neck entry suit with the non-magnetic rings we used to wear. He had a dry suit and wore his super space-age coveralls. However, the outer membrane was so closely woven that it did not allow air migration, so he could not vent his suit to expel the air. As a result he was unable to leave the surface.

A buddy line joined me to him, and I waited on the bottom for him to descend. I was like a little boy holding a balloon, with him floating directly above me, unable to dive. It was a farce, and apart from a large octopus in my torchlight, it was a waste of good breathing air. I aborted the dive and found another partner to dive with.

Night diving has a magic all of its own.

The team, whom I got to know well, had achieved all the diving aims in a difficult environment and we were stronger as a group because of this. I still had severe doubts about the priorities and abilities of the expedition leader to lead in a crisis. One of my golden rules for any expedition is that everyone is equal. There should be no status, other than the skill and knowledge an individual brings with him, which earns the respect of others. If one eats cake, we should all eat cake. However these guidelines were clearly of no consequence and it disturbed me. Upon return from the expedition, and after a lot of soul searching, I wrote to the Expedition Leader and resigned from the expedition. I cited the reasons that I have already mentioned and copied the letter to all of the expedition members. My appointment of Diving Officer was taken over by Mal Strickland, who was previously the Equipment Officer. Mal and I were good friends and he understood my feelings. He was a very capable guy, and I wished him every success for the expedition. I returned to Germany and found that my new posting was back to the military school in Kent. I returned to Folkestone and the channel. It was 1987.

Folkestone, Again: A Bit of Philosophy and All that!

I had been promoted to Warrant Officer Class One and was stuck between two stools. The appointment I was initially selected for was Regimental Sergeant Major (RSM) with London University, but the position would not become available for another year. I was sent to the Royal School of Military Engineering as an instructor. It was the same place I had been before my last tour of Germany. It allowed me to rejoin the eclectic mix of characters and Herberts in the Folkestone Sub Aqua Club. I loved diving out of Folkestone and the craic with the guys.

They were irreverent to rules and authority, which was directly opposite to commercial diving and the Army. As an example, I would like to relate a true story to you.

We were loading onto a Rigid Hull Inflatable Boat in the inner harbour at Folkestone one day, dressed in dry suits and loading kit. A German man approached and asked if he could come diving with us. We said all right and he got changed. The wind was picking up but the forecast was not too bad. However, as soon as we got around the breakwater, the sea was horrendous, two to two and a half metre waves. There was no need to state the obvious, we were not going to dive in such conditions. However, as we were all dressed, we did as we usually did, and went out anyway to check some navigation marks given to us by the fishermen for new wrecks. We gamely chugged out to sea, chatting away.

Underneath the driver operator's seat we kept a crate of beer. The operator stood up and we all grabbed a beer. There was the 'tish' sound of cans being opened and the craic continued. The German lad, who had refused a beer, just watched, boggle-eyed, in silence. Of course, nobody had mentioned publicly that the dive was cancelled. It was unspoken. I could see panic creeping into the German lad's face, especially as some of the guys were already into their second or third beers. The conversation became louder and the jokes got worse. Eventually the German lad could take no more. He sidled up to Timmy and declared in accented pigeon English 'It is very rough, yes?' Timmy took a swig of his beer, looked at him and said 'Rough? Rough? No, this is nothing mate. You should have been with us yesterday. We had to drink Heineken!' I nearly wet myself.

I must, however, say that, even with my background of quite severe military and commercial experience, I was never ever concerned about any aspect of diving with them. They were, for all their irreverence, very competent, able and adept at diving, navigation and boat handling. I was delighted to be part of them, but do not tell them I said so.

The club had found a multitude of additional wrecks, and we set about diving them all. There was a lot of variety, history and adventure with the wrecks. On many of them, the cargoes were still accessible: porcelain, grandfather clocks, champagne, hand painted bowls from Holland, jewellery and ornate brass fittings from first class steamers of times gone by. Nothing was of life changing value, but all were treasures to us.

The good ship Seine sank in 1952 after a collision in fog, carrying a cargo of half bottles of champagne called Golden Guinea, which were made to commemorate the demise of the guinea as legal tender. We brought up hundreds of bottles, and still found it quite drinkable. During one infamous dive, from the beach at Dungeness, we tasted the champagne en route back to shore. It was not only nice, but it was strong. The lads still fondly remember that particular night. A car became trapped in the soft sand and four of the lads were unable to get out of their diving suits. One of them ended up sleeping in a deckchair in his garage. They were halcyon days indeed.

At this time I was offered a military appointment within the Medway area instead of going to London, which I accepted. The new appointment meant that I was able to stay in the same Army house and the children were able to stay at the same schools, without the upheaval of moving to London.

By this time my family had had sixteen moves in twenty years (including the move at five days notice from the Army Diving School) and enough was enough. It also meant that I could continue diving with the Folkestone club, with all their daring-do and expertise in the channel.

Many of the Folkestone lads had never been on an expedition, although a few did attend the Scapa Flow expedition. I thought I would do something about that fact. Whilst I was no longer a military diver, I still retained all of the qualifications and experience and I still used my Sub Aqua Diving Supervisor (SADS) qualification. I had qualified as an Army Diving Supervisor and I some twenty years experience across the three disciplines of diving. I took the Sub Aqua Diving Supervisor responsibility very seriously, and really had no excuse at all for any potential incident.

I continued to dive within the Army Sub Aqua Diving Association (ASADA). In turn, the Army Sub Aqua Diving Association formed an allegiance with the British Sub Aqua Club and followed their rules and diving practice. I was a member of the British Sub Aqua Club as a requirement of the Army Sub Aqua Diving Association, and was a British Sub Aqua Club Advanced Diver. This allowed me to dive anywhere in the world as a recreational diver. I did not need any other qualification to achieve what I wanted to achieve as a recreational diver.

I was a certified commercial and military diving instructor, which has proving exams far more severe than any sport diving organisation, and also included physical and practical tests.

However, I was not allowed to instruct sport diving within the British Sub Aqua Club or sign logbooks. I wrote to two successive British Sub Aqua Club diving officers to explain that I thought I had enough instructional qualifications and sub aqua experience to be allowed to instruct on British Sub Aqua Club courses. The physics of diving is the same no matter where you are in the world.

However, the British Sub Aqua Club is an institution, as is the Army Sub Aqua Diving Association. All institutions have a raft of simplistic rules for members, which is fine for keeping order but stifles initiatives. I was not hopeful, and the fact that I did not receive any answer to my enquiries is indicative of just that. I could see that the British Sub Aqua Club was a business and money was all-important, so I offered to pay the equivalent instructors course fees to the Royal National Lifeboat Institution. I received no response. On the next five expeditions I attended, I went as a Sub Aqua Diving Supervisor and Instructor. These were to Falmouth, Scapa Flow, Kiel, Cyprus and Norway. I gave every lecture and skills lesson in the British Sub Aqua Club programme and copied all the dates and information in a notebook. When I returned a friend of mine who I had trained years before and was now chairman of the Army Sub Aqua Diving Association and a committee member, filled in and signed the logbooks, even though he was not even there. How farcical is that?

It was either do that or cancel the expeditions, as without a Sub Aqua Diving Supervisor, they could not take place. This continued for many years and I have now vetoed myself from instructing. I am due to go on an expedition in four months time to Mombasa, an area I know well where they are desperate for people to instruct, but I have refused. Whilst I am not a fan of institutions and lean a little towards the 'rules are for fools but for the guidance of wise men' philosophy, you get to understand that nothing shoots itself in the foot with more regularity than institutions. The main reason I include this now is to highlight a nonsense. I hold a list of qualifications in diving, in all the three main disciplines; commercial, military and sports. In sports diving I was given the accolade of Diver of the Year in 1981, and I hold the Association of British Diving Schools Class One instructors certificate with the certificate number of 007 (shaken not stirred!). However, non of this is accepted by the British Sub Aqua Club to enable them to award me a certificate of competence as a diving instructor with another agency, which would allow me to instruct within their training programme. So be it. I no longer bother.

However, when one institute (the Army Sub Aqua Diving Association) becomes embroiled with another (the British Sub Aqua Club), they may do it for good reasons, but they become blinkered.

The Army Sub Aqua Diving Association made it compulsory for all its members, or those diving within its association, to become members of the British Sub Aqua Club. It was not cheap. Some guys would, very often, attend an expedition with the sole aim of gaining a basic sports diving qualification. They carried out an intensive course to gain a qualification and then may have remained inactive for several months or years. They had to pay a fifty five-pound initial subscription charge, which was a nice little earner for the British Sub Aqua Club and an arrangement that boosted their coffers and their membership numbers. Whilst I have no argument with the British Sub Aqua Club itself, as it is one of the leading agencies for sport diving, there are others equally prominent as sport or recreational diving institutions.

I may be a bit contentious here but, whilst all sport diving institutions are essentially businesses, and the main aims of all businesses are to make a financial profit, they must keep themselves customer friendly.

To this end, they ignore obesity and fitness in their programmes. They can recommend all they like, but very often obese people pay their money and receive qualifications. Whilst they may have some academic ability to retain simple information and be able to pass a multiple choice test, the fact that they can be morbidly obese or just plain unfit makes a nonsense of their system.

This is totally opposite to all military and many commercial diving courses. Being physically unfit or obese is a certain failure point on all military diving courses and training. In fact, this is the first thing that is tested, and anyone who fails does not even get to unpack their suitcase. Of course, if a business were run on this basis, profits would be affected so they do not do it. Whilst I understand this, I do not agree with it.

During everybody's diving experience, regardless of which discipline they pursue; military, commercial, sport or recreational, there will inevitably come a time when they will be required to physically exert themselves. If they are very unfit and cannot perform as required, they are generally in serious and life threatening trouble.

A few years ago, a sport diving agency ran a training course with the Army in Germany. They were allowed to use the military facilities in the local camp, as most of the students were in the Army. The agency sent over a National Instructor, who was a huge bearded guy weighing about nineteen stone. He was quite full of himself.

I observed whilst he addressed the course, and heard him tell repeatedly how good he was, what the students had to do and how hard they had to work to be like him. It was embarrassing. A colleague next to me whispered, 'I would love to be like him, but I don't think I could eat that many doughnuts!'

Afterwards, there followed a hushed conversation between a few of us not involved, on theme of 'How on earth can that guy expected to be taken seriously?' I mention this as an example of how huge the gap is between sport and military diving.

I read nowadays of many deaths underwater within recreational diving agencies. Many people in their fifties have the money to buy new exotic dive systems, rebreathers, trimix and helium, but the money is all they have. If they had to pass the Army's Basic Fitness Test before they could buy one, I estimate that less then one percent would be sold.

However, market forces govern the shops. It is the same as selling me a Honda Fireblade motorcycle. When I was Olympic fit in my twenties and thirties, I could not afford one. Now I am nearly sixty I can afford it, but I have none of the attributes left; reflexes, eyesight, co-ordination, to be able to ride it safely and successfully. It would probably be the end of me. I am lucky because, during the long journey to reach where I am now, I did all the courses and earned the qualifications, whilst I was young and in my prime. It is now out of my system and I feel that I no longer have anything to prove. If I now tried to become Peter Pan and bought myself a Honda Fireblade or helium rebreather, I hope I have enough good people around me to tell me not to be a bloody fool. And they would be right.

I dive with some great characters, many of which use nitrox and mixtures. They boast to me that they can stay down longer with less decompression. I say 'I know that'. They then ask me 'So what happens to you when you have to leave an interesting dive whilst in the middle of something?' I tell them, 'That's easy, I'll come back tomorrow.' I am now a hobby diver, nothing more, and there is nothing down there that will not still be there the next day.

I had started my new job and had settled in to it. It was mainly desk based, from eight o'clock to four thirty and, almost daily, I would run the country lanes around Kent during my lunch hour. I was at Folkestone almost every weekend, and there was always feverish excitement and anticipation about the dives. Many of the divers had bought their own Rigid Hull Inflatable Boats, so access to and from the dive sites was much faster than with the old 501 motorboat. The Rigid Hull Inflatable Boats were equipped with satellite navigation systems and all modern conveniences. They were like waterborne motorbikes, and distances of up to twenty-five miles to a dive site were not unusual. Compared to the 501 launch, which was ahead of its time for a sport club, travelling the same distances would have taken much longer.

Falmouth

I was still in contact with the military club at Maidstone, which was run by Chris Goddard, an old buddy of mine from way back. Chris had been an Army Advanced Diver during his career.

However, Chris liked diving enough to continue as a sports diver, which was very rare. In fact, he is the only other trained Army diver I know that has become an accomplished sports diver and maintains an active involvement as a recreational diver.

Chris invited me on an expedition with his club to Falmouth. It was a nice expedition to a nice place, but the most important part for me was that my son Gary also attended, as he had qualified as a sports diver with the British Sub Aqua Club. Therefore, we got to dive together and he was able to show his old dad a thing or two. He first dived with me at the age of six and had progressed from there. Now we were on an expedition together. I was very pleased and proud.

We stayed in a local Territorial Army barracks, which was great. Most towns have them, and they usually help out with accommodation for military expeditions. It is mutual scratching of the highest order!

I continued Diving with as much priority and variety as my job allowed. I was nearing the end of my Army career and had to focus on what to do next.

During this time I was asked to instruct on various topics by both Folkestone and Medway Diving Clubs. The subjects varied from drysuit diving to Therapeutic Recompression, and I visited the graving dock at Woolwich for the first time. It was a good example of an old facility being put to good use in the modern world.

Kiel, with the Herberts!

The Folkestone club spent a great deal of time and effort diving on German submarines. We scoured the archives and old reference books for information about them. Some of the U-boats were quite intact and looked wonderful under water. Of course, if they were battened down there was no way anyone could go inside, but some of them had been ripped open by explosive depth charges.

I became fascinated with them. During a well-remembered dive in October 1988 I dived on U55. My buddy was Dave Bachelor, who is now a very experienced dive boat operator in the English Channel. We swam around the wreck and I felt quite strange. I became cold and had a fit of the shivers and felt uneasy. After the dive I mentioned this to Dave, who explained that that particular wreck had a bad history. One of the crew had escaped and had been picked up by a minesweeper. He had told of mass suicides on board, as the batteries had given off chlorine gas. They had tried to use a revolver, but some of the bullets had become wet and the gun would only work some of the time. Then they had to stop the gun falling in the water after the deed had been done. It was a quite horrendous account. I am not superstitious, but I do associate the bad circumstances of that wreck with my feeling of unease. I have never before or since felt the same unease or shivers as I did during that dive.

Another true story about the intrepid Folkestone bunch was when they planned to remove a large phosphor bronze propeller from one of the submarines. The easiest and simplest method was to use explosives. As I had been a member of the Institute of Explosive Engineers for many years, I was asked for advice. I explained that, to hold a licence and to become qualified, they would have to take a course, pass the exams and become a member of the institute. Four of them did just that, and successfully removed the propeller a couple of months later. I think that showed initiative by the boys.

I knew from my time living in Kiel that the town, for Germany, has a very similar role as that of Portsmouth in England. It has an extensive history relating to the German Navy in both shipbuilding and docking.

Today there is a very inspiring edifice on the eastern entrance to Kiel harbour, a large sandstone construction in the shape of a submarine conning tower. It is the marine memorial to the German Navy.

A little further away is the very moving submarine memorial, with the names of all the submarines and crews that were lost. The marine memorial also houses a large museum, which was a source of much valued information, not only about the U-boats in the channel, but also the wrecks of Scapa Flow.

I planned an expedition to Kiel with the Folkestone club. It took place during Easter in 1989. I arranged the accommodation and we booked onto the Harwich to Hamburg overnight ferry. We landed in Hamburg the next morning and drove the eighty miles to Kiel. Even though it was Easter, the weather was bitterly cold. The wind came from the Baltic States in the north-east, and as I had dived under a metre of ice in Kiel in the past, I knew just how the area was affected by the north-easterly winds.

We launched the boats and operated from the British Kiel Yacht Club, which was situated in a little village outside Kiel. It had all the facilities we needed, and we had borrowed an outboard motor and inflatable floppy from the Army. We visited all the historic sights and enjoyed the atmosphere of Kiel.

We only dived a couple of times, once by the main lighthouse and another time at an old weapons dump. We found nothing, but years earlier I had found a Mauser rifle still with its leather sling.

We returned after six days via the Hamburg to Harwich route. We spent the last night in Hamburg's St. Pauli district, a mandatory custom to all visitors there. Whilst the diving was restricted and somewhat uninteresting, the sights, history and war stories made it a memorable trip. Whilst I do not class the

Kiel trip as an expedition in the purest sense, it was a worthwhile experience for the lads. One of the only times they excelled as a team was when, on the last day, they staged a scenario for my benefit. They pretended that they had dropped the borrowed Army outboard motor into the water and started to look for it, putting on a very convincing show. They caught me out, and I was just about to report the loss when they admitted it was only a joke. I had not credited them with such mental agility, and I have to admit I was completely taken in. Bastards!

By this time I was nearing the end of my twenty-two years in the Army. It was time to decide what I wanted to do next and make plans. Some of the Folkestone lads said that they were planning to buy some land as a venture, and asked if I wanted to join them.

They were all Kent businessmen, and I thought that investing in land in Kent had to be a positive step. I went to view the land, which was called Old Wives Leas. It was beautiful chestnut woodland on clay soil, lying between Canterbury and Ashford.

For many years I had been a survival instructor with the military. It was not only a much-loved pastime, but I had practised and experienced it worldwide. Many of the diving expeditions I had attended were in desolate, isolated places, where I had gained experience and knowledge of survival skills. I drew up a small business plan, visited my bank and formed Kent Survival School. I contacted a couple of Army lads who were stationed in the area, and I knew to be suitable and have the right experience to become instructors. We were off. The school ran successfully for more than two years and was very enjoyable.

To my surprise most of our students were married women. However, we taught everyone from cadets, children's homes, small companies and would be soldiers. It was great fun.

I wrote all of the lesson plans and advertising brochures. I adopted the colour green for all our script work, built shelters in the woods for briefing rooms and made and placed field latrines.

I bought a house in Maidstone where we planned to live. Things looked very positive and life was good. Gary had followed in my footsteps and joined the Army as a Junior Leader at Dover, as I had done. Sarah had passed the Eleven Plus exam and was attending Tonbridge Grammar School for Girls, and Paula was coming up to secondary school. We were on an even keel.

All my free time was spent diving in Folkestone and working at the school.

At the beginning I ran a course for journalists from all the local Kent newspapers, which proved very successful and spread the word. One valuable lesson I learned was that, no matter how isolated you think you are in the countryside, anything that you leave outside unattended will get stolen if it has any value, or destroyed if it does not. I find it very difficult to understand that mentality.

I spent three years diving with the Folkestone club, and we had accumulated more than one hundred and eighty local wrecks on which we dived. The Seine, which I have already mentioned, had the cargo of champagne. I was still involved in bringing up bottles for personal consumption, and I featured on the front of the British Army's magazine Soldier, standing chest deep in water wearing diving gear, drinking champagne from a glass. They wrote a very nice article about our exploits at the time.

Back to Germany

I was in the middle of preparing to leave the Army, with literally days left, when, out of the blue, I was offered extended service. This meant staying in the Army until the age of fifty-five. There are many jobs available worldwide for soldiers on extended service. I was offered a job as part of a team running a training area in the north of Germany. I talked it over with Annie. It offered more money than staying in England would have done, and one of the requirements for the job was to be a German language speaker. Having weighed up all the pros and cons, I accepted the offer. I bade a sad farewell to the Folkestone bunch and rented out the house in Maidstone.

We were soon on our way back to Germany. The survival school, which had no overheads, was placed in boxes and stored. The lads had started to offer Paintball as an activity on the land in Kent. When I left they gave me twenty sets of Paintball kit. Later, I started my own Paintball business in Germany for the Army guys. It went very well. I loved my job driving around the training area shepherding the military armoured exercises. There was no training on Sundays to comply with local customs, and very often the troops opted to play Paintball. I had chosen the right sideline business.

Reassurance and Confidence whilst Training

Whilst I have been teaching, training and supervising people to dive for more than forty years, I know it is always important to empathise with how students may be feeling, no matter how easy I think it is or how confident I feel. There is a true story that I always remember about my parachuting career. I only ever did one jump.

It was in 1975 and I was stationed at Maidstone where many of my colleagues were military parachutists. My greatest fear in life is heights. To confront and hopefully overcome this phobia, I decided to take part in a parachute jump. Also stationed at Maidstone was an Army demonstration and freefall team called the Blue Eagles (I think) and they offered a parachute jump for ten pounds. This was quite a lot of money in 1975, but I thought that an easier and more convenient opportunity would surely never present itself, so I signed up to do a jump. It was a two-day course. One day was spent rolling around the gymnasium floor on coconut mats. The next day we drove to an old Second World War airfield in Kent for the jump. Everything was okay so far.

The day in the gym was easy and we learned how to land feet first. That night, because of nerves, I hardly slept at all and kept nodding off in the mini bus on the way to the airfield. When we arrived at the would-be airfield, we found that it was only a grass field with a flattened area at one end and an old metal half-round hut.

We got out of the mini bus and were told to go into the hut and collect our parachutes. I decided that I really needed to get this out of the way as soon as possible, so ensured that I was first through the rickety wooden door, which lay askew on one hinge and rested in some nettles. We entered into the unlit dusty gloom and went up some stairs.

Positioned centrally in the room was a table, and on the far side of it was a member of 'the team' in a bright orange DayGlo jumpsuit. I was first. He was busy chatting to another DayGlo god then, as if it was all a bit of an effort, he went into the gloom to some shelves and came back with a backpack and parachute. As he dumped it on the table there were pinging sounds like poppers on a jacket, and a piece of white silk fabric appeared through a burst opening. He said 'Oh bother, I'll have to repair that. Wait over there.' I picked up the bundle and waited to one side. He served everyone else without any problems. I was now last and holding a bundle of straps, silk and canvas. In a short while, I would be expected to jump out of a perfectly serviceable aircraft with it. Things were not going well. He grabbed hold of my parachute, rammed the silk back into the split and tried to replace the chrome pins through the eyelets.

They kept popping out again, and I watched as he placed a ripcord in them to keep them from undoing. There is usually thin twine to keep the studs in place (called breaking ties), but several of these had snapped (which had caused the popping sounds) so, as a precaution, he had replaced the ripcord and told me to point it out to 'the team' in the 'manifest area'.

'Okay', I said and trundled off to the 'manifest area', which happened to be a blackboard in the middle of the field (obviously no expense spared), and waited to be checked, prior to getting on the plane. A small aircraft had appeared on the grass runway. The side door was missing and you could see right inside the small cockpit. The pilot was wearing a large raincoat and had heavy stubble. He looked more unkempt and dishevelled than Bob Geldof (sorry Bob), and just when you wanted to see a square-jawed, alert, clean shaven hero giving non-stop thumbs up signs, you got this guy. His only movements that I can remember, were a repetitive series of big yawns as he snuggled down into his seat. The noise from the single propeller engine was quite deafening.

My turn came to be checked over. The DayGlo gave me a cursory once over and told me to move forward ready to board the aircraft. I remembered that, in the store, they had put the ripcord in and instructed me to tell him, so I tapped him on the shoulder and said 'I was supposed to show you this'. 'Blimey, where did that come from?' he exclaimed. 'Your mate put it in!' I replied. For those of you who are not as expert in parachuting as I am, those leaving the aircraft independently use the ripcord. They control when the parachute opens by pulling it. The difficult part is remembering the name of the great Indian chief that has to be screamed as you freefall through space towards earth. For those of you who need reminding, it is Geronimo (otherwise the parachute will not open correctly!).

Novice and first time jumpers exit the aircraft using a line called the static line, which is attached to the aircraft and becomes taut, pulling the parachute out of the rucksack. Real experts call this line the dope rope, and not only does it pull out your parachute, but there are no complicated Indian names to remember. Instead, the parachute is kept in the backpack by the breaking ties, which snap under the great pressure, allowing the parachute to spew out (as happened to me in the store).

If, when using a static line, the ripcord is still in place, it prevents the backpack from being opened by the static line, resulting in the parachutist being towed behind the aircraft like a conker on a string.

This had been mentioned the previous day by a DayGlo whilst discussing what can go wrong. The parachuting fraternity refers to a cock up as a mally, which is parachutists' slang for malfunction. We were told that, in the unlikely event of a mally, we should look up to the aircraft and signal our wellbeing to the dispatcher by placing a hand on top of our head. He would then cut the static line, allowing us to free fall through space and open up our reserve parachute before floating gently and safely down to earth. Hmm, sounded a piece of cake to me. One student asked what would happen if someone was unconscious or injured. The

DayGlo replied, 'I'll just swear that you had your hand on your head'. Great, as long as we all know.

I was just about to board the aircraft with my ripcord still fitted. Things were still not going well.

The DayGlo came over and said, 'Stand still', and gave a pull on the ripcord. Nothing happened. He gave a bigger pull but still nothing happened. He then tugged really hard.

I was pulled forward a pace, but still nothing happened. He lost patience, grabbed hold of the ripcord handle, a D buckle, with both hands, put one foot on my reserve parachute on my chest, and gave an almighty tug. The ripcord broke and he fell backwards onto his backside, still holding the D buckle with some loose wire strands hanging from it. I was going to say that I thought, considering he was an instructor, he could have fallen with more skill, but something told me that there was a time and place to be smart, and this was not it.

He found a pair of pliers and disappeared behind me. I heard some snipping and felt the backpack being pulled one way and then the other. He reappeared carrying a tangle of wire and pins and said 'That should do it'. Great!

I then started to look at every body else to see if I could spot any differences. You may remember spot the difference cartoons in magazines. They were quite easy: two feet, two feet; one backpack, one backpack etc (get the picture?). It was then I noticed that my backpack had two lengths of rope dangling from it, and I was the only one who had them. I went up to him and asked, 'Are these important?' He said 'Oh blimey'. They were the lines that were used to attach the bottom of the reserve parachute to the backpack. This was to prevent the reserve from smacking me hard in the face when I left the aircraft, as it was snap-hooked to my harness at the top. It could pivot if it was not restrained at the bottom, which was what the lines were meant to do. Perhaps, if it smacked me hard enough, it would take my mind off trailing after the aircraft on the static line like a conker. Clever people these parachutists.

Things were still not going well.

By this time I was in a kind of zombie state, trying to convince myself that everything was going to be all right. I was not convincing myself at all. I stood with another two guys, waiting for the aircraft to taxi to a stop. As we approached the doorway, the DayGlo in the aircraft gestured for me to look behind. As I did so, I saw the DayGlo at the blackboard beckoning me over to him. I thought 'What the hell does he want now?' I approached him and he shouted in my ear, 'Listen Sarge. When you land, make sure you give your parachute to me personally because it needs repairing!' Things were still not going well.

I trundled back to the aircraft in a daze. The preceding week, I had been promoted to Sergeant. Everyone else on the jump was a junior rank. Not only was I now expected to lead by example, but I knew that showing natural human feelings such as fear and blind panic were just not acceptable. Therefore, I stifled my natural instincts to drop to my knees at the aircraft door, clinging to one of the wheels screaming, 'I don't want to go up!' Although it would have shown what I was really feeling, it would have gone round the Army like a bush fire. It would have done little to my 'hardened veteran overcomes dreaded phobia by doing death defying parachute jump perfectly' image. In addition, I would have had to live with someone, somewhere having a laugh daily. I got into the aircraft resigned to my fate, thinking that it would be pure relief to die. The aircraft took off. To say it was a squeeze on board would be an understatement.

There was the pilot, 'Bob', a DayGlo dispatcher, and three first time jumpers. There was a two-seater bench seat behind the pilot, on which the three of us tried to sit, with the DayGlo in the middle.

In fact I lied. The parachute backpacks had the seats and we were suspended with our backsides in mid air. The other novice knelt on the floor beside the pilot. When we reached a certain height (I do not remember which height, as I was past caring!), the dispatcher had to clip our static lines onto an anchor point, which nobody could see, but was somewhere under the pilot's seat. This was made even more of a challenge by the fact that Bob's flasher mackintosh hung around him and shrouded the seat to the floor like heavy curtains. The dispatcher had to twist his body to get one arm under Bob's seat to attempt to connect the static line. He put his other elbow into my groin with such force that I could not breathe. He looked directly into my face and saw a look that was somewhere between fear of death, panic and asphyxia, and asked, 'Are you all right?' I could not speak, but gave him a benevolent look, which conveyed a 'never been better, thanks', type of message.

The first guy departed, stepping out of the door onto a strut on the wing. He received the 'depart now' slap and off he jolly well went. I was next. On my way to the door I noticed a penknife in the cockpit, which I assumed was there to cut the static line in the event of an impression of the hilarious conker routine.

I can remember feeling the strength of the wind as I stood on the wing waiting to die. Whilst I cannot remember much about the parachute opening, the sensation of floating down was really quite pleasant, perhaps helped by the fact that I was still alive.

I enjoyed floating down and had a little steer by pulling on the straps like all the experts do — and landed on a barbed wire fence!

My relief was immense. As I trundled back to the manifest area, one of the DayGlos approached me and said, 'Great news. We've done a deal with the pilot. For another ten pounds you can have another jump'. I told him to put that jump and all subsequent jumps where the sun does not shine.

My parachuting career was over. I had peaked early and reached the top, changed out of my coveralls, and sat like the expert I was in the mini bus.

I have related this true story to highlight a couple of relevant points. I know that it was not diving related, but there are many parallels with diver training. A general rule of thumb that I use is that any activities that attract DayGlo posers, and parachuting and skiing are prime examples, need to be approached with caution.

The old adage 'All the gear. No idea', is often very true. The DayGlos that I met that day may well have been very good at what they did, but they had absolutely no understanding or empathy with how the other students or I was feeling. They were too busy posing.

Every time I conduct novice training, no matter how sunny, where it is in the world, how clear and warm the water, how easy or old hat I think it is, the student or novice may well be feeling exactly as I was when I did my parachute jump. I am always conscious of that. It helps me remember that it is the students who are the most important ones, and that is how it should be.

Nearing the End

When I started the extended service, my Army career had ended. Anything that I had not done or achieved remained as it was. I finished up a Warrant Officer Class One and that was it. The main thing that the extended service offered was a steady wage, which assisted in planning further education for the kids. It proved to be a prudent decision.

Both Sarah and Paula went on to university, just as the government announced tuition fees. That did not matter. It enabled me to give them the chance that I never had, and I was delighted to do so. Sarah achieved a degree in Geology at Leicester University and Paula achieved a degree in Equine Studies and Business Management at Cirencester Agricultural

College. We managed to support both of these courses of study from my Army salary and my small Paintball venture.

I was also able to continue diving, which I still do today, by using my Sub Aqua Diving Supervisor qualification. I was able to attend and contribute towards many more expeditions. I thought that I would relate some of these here, and hopefully sign off in an amusing way. To those of you who are still awake, well done. With no particular order or priority, here are some small articles on a variety of expeditions I have run and attended since 1990.

Norway, 1991

The Army had set up a base for adventure training pursuits in Norway, near the city of Kristiansand in the south. I had good memories of the place. In 1966 I attended an Outward Bound course there, and the scenery and sights were wonderful. I had canoed around the coast and had stayed for a couple of nights on Survival Island, a rocky island outcrop along a beautiful but barren coast. At the time, I was a newly trained Army Compressed Air Diver (ACAD) and sport diver. I was amazed at the clarity of the water and colours of the sea growths. However, I had no diving kit with me, so I could only enjoy the views from the surface. I had always wanted to return someday.

Well, someday had arrived, and I was asked to drive up to Norway and set up the Army Sub Aqua Diving Association diving base, and run the first of a series of diving expeditions that had booked a slot at the centre. The Army always leaves a basic diver there during the season to look after and maintain the equipment. The lad who was going up with me was called Brad, a newly qualified sport diver. Part of my job was to show him the ropes and set him on an even keel for the season. It really is a plum job for any young lad. You are almost your own boss, you do not have to wear uniform, and you get the chance to become king of your domain. Provided you kept on top of the job, you were much appreciated by the expeditions that came through, and were often treated as one of their own.

Norway is breathtaking. Around every bend in the road is another picture postcard view of stark dramatic scenery. I loved being back. The Adventurous Training Centre consisted of timber huts on the shore of a fjord. During the time that I attended my course, we lived in tents. The divers had a Landrover and trailer, and the centre had a minibus for communal use. This allowed the diving groups to spread their wings and travel along the coast to a variety of dive sites. The whole set up was idyllic. The person who stayed for the season to maintain the kit and provide continuity during the hand overs between expeditions really had a great job. Very often, he would volunteer to do the job again the following season. The danger was that, eventually, they would not want to return to the rigidity of Army life. There are examples all over the world where lads have been used in adventure training centres and have chosen to leave the Army and stay in the local area. Very often, this decision is influenced by them having a local girlfriend and feeling settled. One such person who

I met there was Daz Collum, who had been the Army Sub Aqua Diving Association representative for several years. He had met a girl and decided to stay. Daz and I became good friends, and I found him to be a good diver with invaluable local knowledge. He had also learned to speak fluent Norwegian and was a great asset to us during the setting up of the season. The members of the expedition arrived and I busied myself with checking over their qualifications and experience in their logbooks. Brad showed them around the equipment and they started to carry out pre-dive preparation, such as filling the cylinders and inflating the boats.

Times were good. We carried out a couple of shake out dives, which tested the equipment and encouraged the group to work together and built confidence. They had a mixture of qualifications and experience, and they did not know each other before coming to Norway. Bonding and teamwork was therefore essential. We did the usual fun activity of each contributing to a small kitty, which would go to the person who, in my opinion, had found the most interesting item underwater. This was just a way of livening up any uninteresting dives. As judge, I was ruled out of entering.

During this time, I witnessed a disturbing incident. One of the divers, a sergeant in an infantry unit, surfaced unexpectedly and screamed 'Help me'. I immediately went to him in the safety boat, but when I got there all seemed well. He removed his diving equipment in the water and came into the boat along with his dive buddy, who had arrived at the surface later. Back on shore, I took them both to one side and asked what had happened. The individual concerned said that his air supply had suddenly stopped. I asked if he knew why or how, but he did not. I had checked his kit as he handed it into the boat. He still had plenty of air and his regulator was working. It disturbed me because the fact that he had screamed meant that he had spat his mouthpiece out. This meant that he was liable to inhale seawater, which always ups the ante in such situations, and is a dangerous thing to do. I asked him why he had not buddy breathed from his dive partner's octopus rig (an additional hose with mouthpiece attached to a diver's regulator for use in an emergency), and then ascended together under control. He did not know why.

I have often witnessed how people forget the basic safety drills when under pressure, but this incident still disturbed me. This guy had progressed to being a Dive Leader, which meant he could be given the responsibility for the wellbeing of lesser-trained divers. I told him 'Okay, we'll sort it out and take another look at it when we get back to the boat yard.

I told him that I would buddy with him on a dive into black water and that we would be going quite deep. I said that we would dive in one hour, after we had had a cup of tea, just the two of us. I told him that he should take a torch and that we would be joined together by a buddy line.

During the next hour I ignored him, whilst gathering my kit. I surreptitiously watched him and saw that he was uneasy. He did not know that I had no intention of doing a deep dive with him. We were both already still within repetitive and combined dive times, and to dive shallow dive and then dive deep is bad practice. I could see him becoming more agitated whilst I nominated a boat crew and started to brief them to drop us off on a vertical rock face, which I knew to go down to eighty metres (too deep for air whilst only recreational diving). I told everybody that it was very black and very cold down there, so everyone had to keep their wits about them topside during the dive. I then deliberately went and stood by myself, pretending to fiddle with my instruments. Within a very short time, the guy approached me and said that he did not want to dive. I said that I knew that already and asked him why. He was very honest and said that he was prone to panic attacks and claustrophobia. We sat down together and had a cup of tea. I explained that there never was any intention to dive, and that I only wanted him to confront the problem, which he was doing. I explained that he was being very sensible and doing exactly the right thing. We chatted about it, and it appeared that he had a reputation within his regiment as the diver, and it became a sort of macho front that he had adopted whilst trying to stifle these panic attacks. I praised him for being honest and told him that his diving on this expedition was at an end. I explained that, if he insisted on continuing to dive, he could easily kill himself and anyone else with him. He exhaled two lungs full of air, shook my hand and said, 'Thanks Tony, it's like I have just had a ton weight lifted from my mind.' I told him it was a hard decision, but it had to be made. I said that we would not tell anyone else. I would just explain that I had stopped him from diving because of a suspected burst eardrum, caused during the ascent. I said he could also say the same when he got back to his regiment, so that he could bow out gracefully, whilst on top form.

He remained a good member of the expedition and continued to provide me with a valuable trained hand in the boat. He enjoyed enormously still being a part of the action. He remained an asset and I remember him fondly.

Some weeks later I saw his diving equipment advertised in the forces weekly newspaper. He had left diving with much dignity.

Daz Collum joined us when he could, and introduced me to a wolf fish, which has to be the grumpiest looking fish on the planet (for puritans, I think the wolf fish is actually an eel). I have not seen one anywhere else in the world, and they had a fierce reputation with the locals. We managed a couple of night dives under a jetty, where they were abundant.

During one of the dives in the fjord, I found a pair of gold rimmed spectacles. The area where I found them was where the young outward bounders carried out capsize drills in our canoes. It was easy to see how the spectacles could have ended up there. They looked quite expensive and had very thick lenses. When I returned to Germany, I wrote to the forces newspaper, advertising the finding of the spectacles and offering to send them on if the owner would like to claim them. Paula asked me, 'How would he be able to read the article to claim them?' It was a fair point, smart and funny kid. Nobody ever claimed them.

At the end of the expedition, the team members presented me with a gruesome doll, made from local pebbles, called a troll.

The kitty was won by a diver that had found a very ornate porcelain teapot, whilst diving in the Washing Machine, a gully alongside Lindesnes Lighthouse. On some days, the tidal surge is known to tumble divers down its length. I found a camera lens. During the farewell social, I tried to claim kudos for this fantastic find, but the idea was rejected, so I ended up with the ugly troll. You cannot win them all.

These photos were taken at the same place but 33 years apart. I did an outward bound course at Kristiansands in 1967, and I was the ´Asada` representative on the same spot in 2000. (Don't you just love old age???)

Bornholm, Denmark, 1995

For some reason, the Army had relinquished its Adventure Training Base in Norway. It was a huge loss of a great facility. I believe that the decision was made for financial reasons. For all the superb facilities we had in Norway and the variety of opportunities we were able to provide, it was a shoddy decision. We have never replaced Norway as an Adventure Training Base, yet such a facility provided us with priceless adventure training for many decades.

In 1995 the Army Sub Aqua Diving Association (ASADA) rented a house on the Danish island of Bornholm in the Baltic Sea between Denmark and Sweden. As I was the Equipment Officer, I went up with the initial group to set up the system for the succession of expeditions that were planned.

The Army Sub Aqua Diving Association representative was my son Gary, who would stay up there and tend to the equipment to ensure its serviceability. It was planned that I would only spend a week there and then return to Germany.

I was very proud that Gary had been recognised for his diving skills, and I knew that he would enjoy the summer months up there. We stayed in a holiday home, which was a converted barn and more than adequate.

One of the must do dives in the area was off the northwest coast of the island. There was the wreck of a Russian nuclear submarine, which had sunk during a storm, whilst being towed. It is not often that you get to dive on such a wreck, and I was looking forward to it. As it was several miles out and in deep water, we planned a series of shallower dives to build up to the submarine.

We had an eclectic mix of people up there. There was my old friend Chris, who was then the Chairman of the Army Sub Aqua Diving Association, and we were stationed together in the same place in Germany. There were a couple of Army trained divers. One of them, Nick, was also a recreational diver and had recently arrived on the scene. The other, Mick, was Army trained but had no formal recreational diving qualifications or experience.

An interesting episode occurred on one of the dives. I had been diving from inflatable boats for many years, and at Folkestone we had adopted a system where, at the end of the dive, we would come alongside the boat and, using a large carabiner (snap hook), we would clip ourselves on to the side of the inflatable. Then we would unbuckle our equipment and float free of the equipment. The boat crew would then lift the equipment inboard and stow it. The weight belt would be unbuckled and handed in to the boat under control, instead of being thrown over the tube and on to somebody's foot or diving instruments. It was a very efficient and comfortable way to exit the water.

I adopted the same method in Bornholm. After one dive, I clipped on and was greeted by Mick, the Army diver, who started to lift the equipment out of the water whilst I was still wearing it. I stopped him and showed him the attaching of the snap hook and the unbuckling of the kit, letting myself float free. I then handed him my weight belt and got in to the boat. When all the divers were in the boat, we set off for the next location. I started my post dive routine with my equipment, but it was not there. I checked again but could not find it. I asked Mick to give me a clue as to where he had put my kit. He answered that he had not put it anywhere, because he had not lifted it in. AAAAAAARRRRGGGHHH!!!!!!!!! I stopped the boat and checked where the stainless steel snaphook was still attached to the boat, but no equipment. We retraced the boat's wake to the dive site. Luckily we were in relatively shallow water and found and recovered all of my equipment, undamaged.

This was a good lesson. I had assumed that the methods we used to in Folkestone would be fairly common, but they were not. Mick, the Army diver, had no sub aqua experience and did not realise to lift in and stow the kit for a buddy diver, as we had done for him. It was not his fault, simply a different set of procedures for different divers.

I learned another lesson in Bornholm, during the dive on the Russian submarine. We intended to travel to the site in two boats. When we were loading up at the small harbour, one of the locals approached me and asked for help. He had lost an anchor but knew exactly where, and asked if I would pop down and put a line on it for him to recover it.

This is a fairly common occurrence when diving, as I have mentioned before. This sort of mutual scratching can help to build a rapport with the local community, and I always try to oblige if I can. Nothing in life is simpler than that.

I popped my equipment on and said that I would do it, but he had to show me exactly where the anchor was. I told the guys that I should only be ten minutes. I descended at the place where he said the anchor was, but nothing was there. There was a metre of coal dust and it was pitch black, so I started to go into it, but still found nothing. I surfaced and he suggested I should try a little to the right. I descended again and had another truffle hunt in the coal dust but still found nothing. I surfaced again and he had another change of mind about the location, but enough was enough. I still had an important dive to do, so I gave my excuses saying that if we had the chance later we would look for it again.

I loaded my kit in to the boat, but it was filthy. Both the kit and I were covered in coal dust. It was everywhere, in my hood, in my mask and in my ears. Down my neck seal and up my wrist seals I was completely black. The reason for the existence of so much coal dust was that a coal tanker had docked and unloaded its cargo for the previous one hundred years. It took three showers before I felt clean again. However, even more important, I had consumed more air than I wanted to, and whilst en route to the Russian submarine, I made the decision that I had insufficient air pressure for a deep dive on to an unfamiliar wreck site. I therefore said that I would supervise, thus allowing the nominated supervisor to dive in my place. He would be able to use the cylinder that was kept for the standby diver. I had enough air left for my equipment to be used as the standby diver set.

There was a good chance that I could have dived safely with the air I did have, but, if there was a problem and someone needed to buddy breathe from my octopus, it was doubtful that I would have enough air to support them. Therefore, I did not dive the Russian submarine.

Gary did dive and enjoyed it, and that was as pleasing for me as if I had dived it myself.

It still remains the best dive I never did!

When it came time for me to leave the island and return to Germany, I became Mr. Bean, and returned from the ferry terminal twice to collect things that I had forgotten from the accommodation (one of them was my passport). It was a catalogue of forgetfulness, for which you could have sold tickets.

It was dawning on me fast that I was well over forty years old. In Army terms that is totally ancient, antediluvian even. To the young lads I was with, I was a considered a dinosaur. This is another comparison with civilian recreational dive clubs. It is not unusual to have divers in civilian clubs that are well into their sixties and seventies, and they continue to be active and usually receive the kudos and respect deserving of their age and experience. In the Army it is the exact opposite. Anyone over the age of forty is considered to have no right to be alive, let alone be on an expedition. My Mr. Bean act of forgetfulness was just a reminder to me that I was getting old. To the youngsters it was the onset of senility.

Cyprus

My diving association with Cyprus has been varied constant and numerous. In many ways it is an ideal location, particularly for diving, diver training and expeditions. You will have heard about it as a site for a military engineering project, earlier in the book. It has a superb climate and the military utilise the location to its fullest potential.

Located in Cyprus is a pool of diving equipment and an adventure training centre. The main character for diving equipment maintenance and training is a guy called "Peds" Pedley. Peds is a product of being an army rep in Cyprus, whilst he was a soldier in Germany. He liked the job and situation so much that he managed to extend his tour out there and then reached the stage of no return and left the army and now does the job as a civilian. He is a very competent and multi qualified individual and a great contact to have.

Of the times I have visited there, all of them were to train and supervise divers. A task that I was often asked to perform was to organise a days recreational diving to dive on the wreck of the "Zenobia". This was a modern new car ferry which due to a computer fault, filled with water and slid to the bottom. It now lies on its port side just outside Larnaca harbour and still looks in pristine condition. Large trucks which were part of the cargo are still chained to the vehicle deck, hanging lopsided precariously on the chains. The top rail of the ferry is at 17/18 metres and provides an ideal safe dive by descending down a line and swimming gently along the handrail, with superb water visibility enabling divers to look over the side rail at the ships upper decks without going deep or penetrating the inside of the wreck.

Often I would be given an assortment of lads with a whole variety of qualifications and experiences. They would be trained worldwide by a multitude of different agencies, usually whilst at a location they would do a standard basic diving course and be given a piece of paper to show their achievement. On such occasions whist motoring out to a dive site, I would question them each in turn about what they had achieved and where they had achieved it. I would check any paperwork they had or question them in the absence of paperwork, looking for clues to verify their competence.

Many of the guys had qualifications with the Professional association of Diving Instructors, (PADI) pronounced Paddy, which they had gained usually in the USA or Canada. I would form diving groups of those who had done their training with the same agencies and were at a similar standard.

I remember vividly ,on one occasion after briefing one of the PADI groups on the dive when one of them raised his hand to ask a question. When I asked him "what?" He said "Why do you keep calling me Paddy, I'm not from Ireland !!!!!".

Such a subtle clanger told me in a heartbeat that he was blagging about his qualifications, so he sat on the boat and sunbathed.

These trips, apart from keeping me fully on my toes, were very rewarding and worthwhile. It was always good to see lads who were taking a well earned break in between hard physical training in extreme heat, have a smile on their faces after an enjoyable dive followed by a cold beer.

Another of my expeditions in Cyprus entailed acting as a sub aqua diving supervisor SADS, for a group of Ghurkhas who had flown in from their base in England. Two of them had attended and passed the Army Compressed Air Divers course at the Army diving school, but none of them had any recreational diving experience. During their two weeks on the island they all attained the qualification of Sports diver, which included a couple of exams which they all passed comfortably.

You can correctly assume that my knowledge of Ghurkhali, is nil, therefore all the instruction, lectures and exams were in English. So my hat's off to them for their achievement whilst doing so in a foreign language. They are truly remarkable, willing and likeable people.

A true story about a Ghurkha student on a military diving course, happened whilst I was an instructor at the Army Diving School. Whilst I was not the supervisor on that course, the story is true. He was diving from a pontoon and was in the water and at the surface, doing mask clearance drill whilst wearing a full face mask. This entailed flooding the mask with the smelly pea green sea water on the surface for all to see, then descending down the shotline, clearing the mask and then returning topside to show the cleared mask. (It was done by breaking the outer seal with two fingers under the chin, then leaning your head back and to one side, exhaling with a blast down your nose and forcing the water passed your fingers on the seal.) This individual had had 4 attempts at it but had not quite managed to clear the mask completely. Giving him a hearty vote of gusto the supervisor told him that this was the one and to give it all he had. He was told to fill his mask again, when he gestured to the exit ladder and proceeded to ascend it, when his knees were out of the water and he was held by his attendant and lifeline, he removed his mask and with great sincerity said to the supervisor, "Sorry sir, I just can't drink any more".

One thing which is very apparent around the island is that the surrounding water is devoid of fish, animal and plant life. It is fished out to a state of being barren. Not only is there hardly any sea life but there is no natural habitat to support them. All the reefs are dead. Often I would see a tin can or small piece of debris lying on the bottom which had been colonised by a few small fish. It gave me the idea to get the numerous groups of divers, courses and expeditions to construct an artificial reef for the local government, using old car tyres and concrete anchors, (locally made).

This would give a useful second life to car tyres, remove them from the rubbish chain on the island and produce a useful and practical resource to help re-populate the depleted fish stocks by giving them a habitat and protective environment to live in. Each group of divers would be responsible for an amount of tyres to be laid.

The whole thing could be overseen jointly by the Army and the local authorities and we divers would be putting something back for the future generations.

Sadly the idea never materialised and I felt that we had missed a great opportunity as divers to contribute and leave behind something useful and worthwhile. (I still think this).

It would also give recreational divers a fulfilling activity to do under water instead just wasting good breathing air.

Cyprus remains a favourite destination of mine. My list of the ten most favourite restaurants in the world, two of them are on the island but I don't tell you where.

There is also a couple of my favourite bolt holes on this planet, which I will also keep a secret. This book would not have been complete without a mention of Cyprus its people, its climate and its diving.

Summary

The book is coming to an end. There are other places and experiences that could have been included, Australia, Medes Islands and a life changing visit to beautiful Borneo. However, enough is enough and to quote a famous quote, "always leave them wanting more". It's not easy just to pull the plug and to end with "I'm soaking wet after my last dive, that's it – goodbye".

My Folkestone buddies suggest that I should put some "shark fights" in and some behind "enemy lines" action, just to beef it up. There were no shark fights and if I have any say in things, there isn't going to be any.

I have witnessed enormous changes in both travel and diving during the last 45 years. The world is getting smaller and places are becoming more accessible. In most of my early travels there was no local support or remedies for dealing with problems, you were often totally isolated.

You had to plan to deal with all eventualities yourself, which made planning, execution and surviving, much more difficult. This installed my grounding for my survival training which I did worldwide and used as a basis for running a professional survival school in later years .

Nowadays civilisation is much closer and accessible. Communications, Navigation and basic living equipment is excellent and by using this technology and equipment correctly, there is no need for any group or individual to be lost or to suffer prolonged distress. The progress also made with airdrops, helicopter operations and satellite location beacons have made adventurous pursuits much safer.

Diving equipment has also changed. There is nowadays a much wider variety of equipment to suit the more diverse tastes and climates. I don't think that this necessarily makes for safer diving now. The old kit was quite reliable if you looked after it OK. The component which was, is and always will be the biggest danger to safe diving, is the diver themselves. Most accidents result from divers underestimating the dive and conditions and overestimating their own ability. As long as this continues there will always be accidents. I read nowadays of unexplained fatalities of divers whilst underwater. If and when the bodies are recovered, the equipment is usually found to be working OK, so how do you explain the deaths?

In all the main disciplines of diving, Military, Commercial and Recreational, the latter two are based on making financial profit.

The Military have no interest in making a profit but find it necessary to make high levels of physical fitness a major priority. It is the only one of the three codes which makes inadequate physical fitness a disqualifying factor from attending or passing a diving course. The Army's basic diving course still has the highest percentage failure rate of any of the army's courses. However the regime can be harsh and brutal which can kill enthusiasm for diving as students associate the diving with getting beasted and exhausted and it doesn't have to always be like that.

Both Commercial and Recreational codes are run as businesses. They need to be if not "warm and cuddly" then certainly user friendly.

If they became too difficult then people will take their money elsewhere.

The Military and Commercial students also require a much stricter medical examination. They have robust training regimes and timetables and have to adhere to a course programme. The intake of knowledge leading to the passing of written exams and practical tests where each phase of training is proven and tested. All training is done whilst under close supervision from the surface. Divers are nearly always in communication with either the surface, each other, on an umbilical or lifeline. Whilst this at times can be inconvenient to carry out certain tasks, it allows for the supervisor topside to continually assess and monitor the divers well being and condition. This in turn leads to being able to diagnose early, any problems or symptoms and take action accordingly.

The Recreational diver can still receive, competent training and diving, providing they pay the required money. However there is a philosophy that there is no need to rough it and I have seen training and lessons effected by the weather or convenience. This is the direct opposite to the Military who use the philosophy of, "If it ain´t raining, it ain't training", and "if it ain´t snowing, we ain't going". (No pain, No gain, we all know).

This tough outlook doesn't always prove to be the best way, as I highlighted in the book, we were banned from wearing gloves or mitts for many years until the realisation dawned that a diver who loses the use of his hands because of hypothermia is no use to anyone, especially himself.

The Recreational diver whilst doing his diving will tend to do it when the weather is good and the water calm, and why not indeed. Whilst they generally have a sensible code of practice, this can tend to go very wrong. I have seen many incidents where Recreational divers have become separated and do things which just get them sliding deeper and deeper into a serious situation. Running out of breathing air, having to surface immediately, losing your buddies or poor dive planning, etc. I know that to make mistakes is only human, but diving at times is a very unforgiving pastime and produces incidents that require stamina and physical fitness to survive, especially with no direct access to safety, that a lifeline or umbilical would provide. If the individual is very unfit, then breathlessness, or hyperventilation, or shallow breathing can occur leading quickly to exhaustion, unconsciousness, deepening into death.

Another consideration, particularly with the Recreational diver, is the pushing of the boundaries on depths and mixtures. The smaller the boundary the less room for error. Remember the Honda Fireblade? Another activity which has advanced in leaps and bounds is underwater photography. In days when I was doing photography you didn't see your results for weeks. Many places I dived were so isolated that there was no photographic developing facilities. So we had to send our films back to the UK and get them resent back to us. Only then could we see the results and see what we were doing right or wrong. Trying to remember what 'F' stop I used and what the general light conditions were at the time, to gain from experience, was very difficult. I have not long returned from diving in the Red Sea where the guys from the Folkestone club used digital cameras and could see the results whilst still on the dive. In Mombasa we did have our own made lab, where we did our own developing and printing. However the advances in underwater photography have been simply breathtaking.

I have been fortunate to have been qualified in all three major diving codes and I have a passion for going underwater since I was 15 years old at Dover. As you have read in this book it has been and still is my main passion. As you will also have read it has given me much variety, excitement and travel. Many of my achievements were due to good teaching. I met many great characters and as I have already stated, " I stood on the shoulders of giants".

I was once asked by a parachutist, how I felt about deep diving in the cold black sea as compared to parachuting from great heights. My answer to him was logical, simple and very true, "If I get into trouble whilst diving, I can swim a few strokes but, I can't fly an inch".

Glossary of Terms and Conditions

APC: Armoured Personnel Carrier.

Aqualung: A device which allows a diver to breathe on demand from a source of high pressure air. Credited with being invented by J Cousteau.

Bale Out: A system which allows a source of breathing air for a diver during an emergency ascent.

CO: Commanding Officer, usually of a regiment/battalion strength

CSB: Combat Support boat.

Cupola: Round access hatch into an armoured vehicle which sometimes incorporates a class scope for external vision.

Demand Valve: Another name for Aqualung.

Ditch Set: When a diver releases his diving equipment whilst under water.

GOC: General Officer Commanding, usually of a large number of units, i.e. a division.

Gun whale: The top rim/edge of a boat.

Jackstay: Length of cordage laid underwater to assist the diver, usually with direction in poor visibility.

Lifeline: A length of rope attached to a diver and tended from the
surface.

Live aboard: A dive boat with accommodation for the divers

Marking Time: A drill move which means, staying in the same spot.

NCO: Non Commissioned Officer,

O Rings: Ring shaped rubber washers used as seals.

OBM: Outboard Motor.

OC: Officer Commanding, usually of a company/squadron strength.

Octopus Rig: A system which allows another diver to breathe from
another divers air supply.

Over the horizon drop off s: Method of dropping divers into the water
for clandestine operations without being visible.

Pass Off : A formal parade in the services to denote the progression of recruits to being fully trained.

Passed In: A term used for the formal acceptance of individuals into the forces, usually in the form of a parade.

Posted: A move, to your next duty station.

Postings: The placing and sending of soldiers to their duty station.

RCC: Recompression Chamber

Rhib's: Rigid hulled inflatable boats.

SCUBA: Self Contained Underwater Breathing Apparatus.

Shot Rope/Line: A vertical weighted line used by divers to descend or ascend in the water.

SIU: Suit inflation Unit.

Standard Diver/Diving: The use of a copper/brass helmet diving equipment, usually associated with older diving tasks.

Surface Demand: A system where a diver breathes air supplied directly from the surface.

Topped Up: When a diver in a dry diving suit experiences the ingress of water to saturation.

Acknowledgements

When I began this book, I wrote it in pencil onto a jotting pad. To get from that first draft to the sleek publication you have just read takes much time, knowledge and professional dedication. I am eternally thankful and indebted to: Susanne Ihde, Helen Astwood and Sarah Davies, for their enormous help and advice over all the stages whilst producing this book especially their typing and computer skills. Thank you all very much.